Worship Musician!

Presents

TIPS FOR
TIGHT TEAMS

TIPS FOR TIGHT TEAMS

High-Performance Help for Today's Worship Musician

Sandy Hoffman

Hal Leonard Books
An Imprint of Hal Leonard Corporation

Published in 2012 by Hal Leonard Books
An Imprint of Hal Leonard Corporation
7777 West Bluemound Road
Milwaukee, WI 53213

Trade Book Division Editorial Offices
33 Plymouth Street, Montclair, NJ 07042

Except as indicated, all scripture taken from the HOLY BIBLE, NEW KING JAMES VERSION. Copyright © 1979, 1980, 1982 Thomas Nelson, Inc. Used by permission.

Scripture quotations from THE MESSAGE. Copyright © by Eugene H. Peterson 1993, 1994, 1995, 1996, 2000, 2001, 2002. Used by permission of NavPress Publishing Group.

Printed in the United States of America
Book design by Mayapriya Long, Bookwrights

Library of Congress Cataloging-in-Publication Data
        Library of Congress Cataloging-in-Publication Data
Hoffman, Sandy.
  Tips for tight teams : high performance help for today's worship
musician / Sandy Hoffman.
      p. cm.
  Includes bibliographical references and index.
 1. Contemporary Christian music--Vocational guidance. 2. Church
music--Handbooks, manuals, etc. I. Title.
  ML3187.5.H64 2012
  264'.2--dc23
                        2011050027

ISBN 978-1-45840-291-2
www.halleonardbooks.com

Play skillfully with a shout of joy.

Contents

Foreword

Sandy Hoffman is the real deal—a polished musician who has successfully mentored his worship teams not only in matters of fine musicianship, but also in matters of the heart. His practical approach and solid ideas are surpassed only by his love for God and others. Just read any part of this book, and you will quickly get a glimpse into who Sandy Hoffman really is, and more important, Whom he serves with all of his heart.

Drawing from literally 30 years of experience, Sandy comes to the table with inspired teaching for you as a worship leader and for your entire worship team. Throughout *Tips for Tight Teams*, your team will be learning how to function in their respective worship roles and enjoy the experience along the way.

Sandy has written for my magazine, *Worship Musician!*, for over seven years now, and when I read each issue, I always sit back and say to myself, "He has done it again!" Every article he writes is filled with richly practical and deep content for worship teams. Blessed with a keen sense of humor, this well-traveled worship leader/teacher takes you to a much better place as a musician, a team player, and a worshiper of Christ.

Tips for Tight Teams is a book bathed in prayers that you and your worship team will rise to the occasion and step into what the Lord has called you to do: minister as a team of skilled musicians in the house of the Lord.

Bruce Adolph
Publisher, *Worship Musician!*

Preface

The goal of *Tips for Tight Teams* is to elevate the skill level of your worship team to the point where it is no longer a distraction to the people it endeavors to lead into worship.

As a lifelong musician, it has always been my belief that if you practice, practice, practice, you will become extraordinary at what you do. The logical rule appears to be: "*You* apply the perspiration, *they'll* apply the praise." This is a true statement, and in most performance applications, praise is the reasonably expected return for the hard work you have invested. In fact, the more effort you put into almost *anything*, the greater the expectation and likelihood of fame and acclaim. But is it possible, in some areas of life, that recognition should not be considered the big payoff? Perhaps a more noble and selfless motive could be in order. Suppose we agree to make it the ultimate goal of good worship musicianship to draw attention to Someone other than self, to decrease in order that He might increase? Now we're talking worship!

Since its inception in the late 1990s, the purpose of the *Tips for Tight Teams* curriculum has been to raise the skill level of the worship team musician. This goal does not exist so that the individual might be noticed and adulated, but rather so that their skills might become polished and refined to the point where they are no longer likely to present an obstacle to worshipers. When worship team *blunders* and *clams* begin to disappear, the attention of the worshiper can be consistently drawn to a higher place, with a sharper focus. We cease to be our own worst enemies in worship, having opted instead to pay the obligatory dues for attaining worship excellence. That's what *Tips* is all about.

Each of the sections in *Tips for Tight Teams* originated in the pages of *Worship Musician!* magazine, to which I have been a regular contributor since 2004. Over the years it has been my pleasure to explore with readers such diverse topics as arranging worship songs, creating a seamless worship flow, developing high-level worship skills, harmonizing team vocals, improvising by inspiration, practicing team dynamics, reading and writing worship charts, transposing keys for ease in worship, and warming up well for worship. We've had a look at everything from meltdowns to missions and modes to modulations. Along the way we've discovered, defined, and yes, even invented words like *schmaltzification* and *mellifluity*. Deep discussions have ensued over such theoretical matters as *encomiastic responses* and the multiplicity of *Ways to Praise*. And yet the readers and I are *still* very good friends after all these years. What a blessing!

Although it is quite thorough, *Tips for Tight Teams* is really very basic. Addressing both worship expertise and sensitivity, it is filled with the worship team essentials called for by our 21st-century worship communities. I like to call it "What you need to play and lead." It is my hope and prayer that you'll feel the same way as you apply the *Tips*, becoming better equipped to be and do what God created for you!

TIPS FOR
TIGHT TEAMS

Part I

THE PATH TO PRACTICING PRAISE

1

Team from the Top

I Wanna Worship!
(But Where Do I Begin?)

Admit it—even if you've never strummed a chord in your life, you'd love to be on that stage with the worship team! There's just something exhilarating about the thought of standing up there, eyes raised to Heaven, worshiping before the people. Skilled and confident, you draw from years of experience as you follow the Holy Spirit into the presence of God. The moment you strike that first *power chord*, a spontaneous psalm explodes from your lips:

> *Oh, sing to the Lord a new song!*
> *Sing to the Lord, all the earth.*
> *Sing to the Lord, bless His name;*
> *Proclaim the good news of His salvation*
> *from day to day.*
>
> —Psalm 96:1, 2 (NKJV)

And you're off! Except for one thing: didn't we just establish that you've never actually strummed a chord in your life? Perhaps then there's a bit of preparation to be done before you reach that fevered pitch of pinnacle praise!

We're History!

Music and worship must be extremely important to the Lord. The scripture says in Genesis 4 that Jabal was the father of those who dwell in tents and have livestock. His brother's name was Jubal. He was the father of all those who play the harp and flute. This is the time when men and women began praying and worshiping in the name of God. As worship musicians, it's our profound privilege to take our place in history alongside those who have lifted up the name of the Lord for thousands of years. Properly applied, the following five steps will help you move from worship dreams to worship teams. You're only a beginner once. The rest, as they say, is history!

1. Get on It!

There's an old saying that goes something like this: "Ninety-nine percent of success is just showing up." Sometimes you can stack the deck by simply getting into the game! To become a worship team member, you have to count the cost, make a plan, and work systematically until you've reached your (and God's) goals. To be a 21st-century *Levite* will take work and determination. But remember what they say: "The harder you work, the luckier you get" (not that I really believe in luck). Doors will start to open, opportunities will present themselves, and if you've done your homework, you'll be ready to meet those opportunities head-on when they come.

2. Purchase an Instrument

Oh! No matter how many years you've been at it, this is the most fun part: buying a new *axe*. With the ability now to research products on the Internet, you can pretty well ascertain the cost, quality, warranty, and bells and whistles of your new instrument before you even try out the real thing. Probably the most important advice to keep in mind when buying your first guitar, keyboard, bass, or drums is to buy the best you can afford. Believe me, many aspiring worship musicians have been severely frustrated by sore fingers, crackling connections, clanging cymbals, and out-of-control controls! The better the instrument you start with, the greater the likelihood of your hanging in there. My grandmother always said, "You get used to hanging if you hang long enough!" Don't give up, but patiently and systematically work at your new skill until it becomes your own. Begin with the best instrument you can afford, and you will never regret it.

3. Learn the Basics

We've all heard the "old lady Crump" horror stories of piano lessons gone bad! The mean ol' teacher anxiously hovering, awaiting the opportunity to strike our tender young knuckles with her ruler when we've made a mistake. Ouch! Thankfully, things have changed. Not only are we surrounded by kinder, gentler teachers, but we also have an almost unlimited selection of books, CDs, DVDs, and downloads available for learning worship techniques in the comfort (and relative safety) of our own homes. DVDs don't talk back, and they don't whack your knuckles! What a relief.

4. Watch the Team

Most worship leaders are more than happy to have you observe them during rehearsals. Perhaps you could even take your instrument and quietly play or sing along with them. In this way, you can begin to accumulate a repertoire of worship songs. You'll have your own collection of *charts* before you're even ready to join the team. Hanging out with other worship musicians also gives you time to build relationships. Look for opportunities to participate in team prayer and discipleship as well.

5. . . . And Own It!

Think your *chops* are up to snuff? You're ready for the team? There are two approaches you can take to find out. First, you could call the worship director, claim to be the next "Stevie Way Wrong" and just dive head-first into the deep end. If you're really that good, there won't be any sinkage. You'll float just fine. However, most of us are more comfortable getting into the water gradually, one toe at a time. Why not begin by volunteering to sub for the person who plays your instrument on the team? Perhaps that individual might become your *mentor* or private teacher. Over time, you'll find your confidence growing and your ministry opportunities multiplying. Who knows—you may even end up being a regular on the team!

The conclusion is this: though it only took you a couple of minutes to read this section, the process of moving from nonmusician to team player can take months or years. Be patient with yourself and others. Walk humbly, ready to receive input and instruction. Before long, you will own it. Remember that worship equals servanthood, and Biblical references to worship are laced with poignant terms like *living sacrifice*. It is our reasonable act of worship to submit *all* to Jesus. When we do that, He faithfully multiplies our blessings back to us in every life situation, even when we *just* wanna worship.

No Expectations?

A man's heart plans his way, but the Lord directs his steps.

—Proverbs 16:9 (NKJV)

A very wise personnel director I know had a most peculiar habit. There was always a lot of energy and electricity in the room before the start of our weekly ministry meetings. With impeccable timing, he would wait until the department heads had all taken their seats around the boardroom table. Without a word, he'd walk to the front of the room, pick up a marker, and very meticulously write these two words on the board: NO EXPECTATIONS. When he turned around, revealing what he'd written, everyone would chuckle, recognizing the spirit in which the direction was given. The meeting would then come to order.

This scenario played out week after week, and it provoked me to ponder the significance of the admonition. Many years have passed since then, and I've finally arrived at two conclusions:

1. A person with no expectations runs little risk of disappointment.
2. A person without expectations cannot easily differentiate between his successes and his failures.

Willing to Risk?

Knowing we may risk some disappointment, let's take a few moments up front and honestly consider some of our worship expectations together. It may have been good to shelve my expectations during those brief departmental meetings so long ago, but I believe that in the greater scheme of a worship lifestyle, it's important to first identify what we expect to accomplish, and second to prepare ourselves for the feedback we'll get, both from those we're leading and from the Lord Himself.

Healthy Worship Expectations

To paraphrase Proverbs 16, "The Lord allows our hearts to make plans, then He directs our plans into His perfect will." In order to develop healthy worship strategies (expectations), we need to answer lots of questions in the following vein: What do we expect when we come together to offer our praises to God? What does the experience of corporate worship look like to me? How do I know I'm truly connecting with God? Should I expect to *feel* anything during worship? How does the experience of corporate worship affect my personal daily walk with God?

These questions are provocative, and should cause us to closely examine our approach to praise. The answers will help us to know whether we're reaching our goals as lifestyle worshipers, lead worshipers, worship programmers, or worship musicians. Let me encourage you to wrestle with these questions and apply the answers to your daily worship life, to benefit both you and the people you lead.

Balance Your Worship Diversity

Psalm 131:2 (NKJV) says: *"Surely I have calmed and quieted my soul."* In contrast, Psalm 35:18 (NKJV) says: *"I will give You thanks in the great congregation; I will praise You among many people."* Are your expectations of worship at one extreme or the other, or do they fall comfortably in the center, with a good balance of both quiet personal reflection and exuberant public exaltation? Do you prefer to kneel reverently before the Lord (Psalm 95:6), or does your expression of praise look more like King David's leaping and whirling before God and all the people (II Samuel 6:16)? That is to say, there is no real limit to how we may be inspired to worship God or to the results we may experience from our worship. There are no worship absolutes. The important thing is to be open to Divine inspiration, expecting to worship the Lord in whichever way is pleasing to Him at the moment.

God's Response

We've seen in just a few short verses the many diverse expressions of worshiping God. This is just the tip of the iceberg. After we've presented our praises *to* God, we have to wonder what kind of response we should expect *from* Him. Does God respond to my worship? Psalm 22:3 (NKJV) says: *"But You are holy, who inhabit the praises of Israel."* Here God lived in the praises of His people! II Chronicles 20 tells the story of the worshipers who went out before the army as they were saying, *"Praise the Lord, for His mercy endures forever."* What was God's response in this context? He caused their enemies to turn against one another, annihilating all three of the armies who had gathered to defeat King Jehoshaphat. In Acts 16, as Paul and Silas were in prison *"singing hymns to God,"* the Lord caused an earthquake, broke them out of jail, and saved the jailer and his whole family. Does God respond to the praises of His people? A resounding yes! Should we expect to experience God's response as we worship Him in the 21st century? Again, yes.

Three-Way Expectations

Our worship expectations can be divided into three categories: God's, yours, and mine. As we look forward to spending time in worship with our growing Christian family, it's appropriate to ask ourselves questions and expect Godly responses. Prayerfully seeking answers will bring us to a foundational understanding of how God sees us in worship, how we perceive one another, and how each of our individual worship gifts combine to become one powerfully anointed, unified voice of praise.

Answers to these worship questions will also help to forge our future worship expectations. Because of God's faithful answers to our questions, during our worship times we can expect to see lives changed, people saved, people healed, relationships restored, God glorified and honored, body unity facilitated, repentance provoked, and forgiveness offered (both vertical and horizontal). Will there be possibilities for disappointment? Yes, but without expectations, we cannot even begin to recognize results.

As you read through *Tips for Tight Teams* and contemplate your expectations of worship, may the Lord grant you wisdom and understanding in the knowledge of His desire for you. No expectations? Hardly.

2

Live the Life
(Through Team Mission
Based on Biblical Principles)

Empowered, Engaged, and Excellent
(All to the Glory of God!)

Now here's a chance to change the Church, and while we're at it, the world! Our local worship ministry, "First Light," has just adopted a fresh, new mission statement. I'd like to share it with you!

The mission of the First Light Worship Ministry is to be spiritually empowered, relationally engaged and musically excellent, all to the glory of God!

Yes! If we strive for "the three Es" in this new mission statement, I believe we'll see substantial increases in our spiritual authority, relational effectiveness (both vertically and horizontally), and musical ministry impact. Empowered, engaged, and excellent—all to the glory of God! These are the areas we're embracing as our worship ministry looks to the future. How about you?

Why Mission?

Do we really need a worship team mission? Can't we just meet, rehearse, and lead worship like we've always done? One of my favorite mission clichés is: "If you don't know where you're going, any road will get you there." It's true. Success is often contingent upon direction, and direction can be clearly communicated through mission statements. When we agree as a team (band) to pursue like-minded direction, our fruitfulness becomes quantitative. It takes on a measurable quality. This builds enthusiasm and infuses our team with a sense of accomplishment. A clear mission gives us both a direction and a destination.

Elements of Mission

There are two non-negotiable elements of a good mission statement. These are based on the answers to some simple questions: Who are we, and what are we doing? In the case of a worship ministry mission, our answers are rooted in motivational Biblical principles. Who are we? We are a "spiritually empowered, relationally engaged, and musically excellent worship ministry" (spoken in faith!). Doing what? "Giving glory to God." Our mission is simple yet profound, as we consider the underlying possibility of reaching these lofty goals together!

A well-crafted mission is also *hooky* and memorable. Run-on statements are hard to recall and are therefore unlikely to be realized. Using devices like the three Es (empowered, engaged, and excellent) helps to make our team mission more easily repeatable.

Biblical Overview

The First Light team based its fresh direction on the following three Scripture passages. As you consider your team mission, I encourage you to first spend time in prayer and the Word, trusting the Lord to "direct your paths" (Proverbs 3:5, 6).

1. Spiritually empowered: ". . . *to be strengthened with might through His Spirit in the inner man*" (Ephesians 3:16b, NKJV)
2. Relationally engaged: "*Oh, magnify the Lord with me and let us exalt His name together*" (Psalm 34:3, NKJV)

3. Musically excellent: *"Sing to Him a new song; play skillfully with a shout of joy"* (Psalm 33:3, NKJV)

Once we agreed upon these Bible bullet points, we expanded on each, bringing clarity and understanding to the mission.

The essence of Christianity is Divinely inspired relationship.

Spiritually Empowered

To be spiritually empowered is to be energized and equipped by the very Spirit of God. Energized means we're enthused, stirred up, and passionate, because His Spirit is in us. We can hardly wait for the next opportunity to stand in the congregation, and lead others into His high praises.

Because He also equips those He calls, we're outfitted, prepared, and taught by His Spirit. Always ready at a moment's notice to "go public," we give an exuberant account of the hope that is in us!

By *"acknowledging and appropriating His power"* (Ephesians 6:10-18), we can accomplish His will and calling on the team. As lead worshipers, our heart is always to motivate the people to honor Him. This happens not by our own clever means, but by His strength, which works in us to the benefit of others.

Relationally Engaged

The essence of Christianity is Divinely inspired relationship. In right fellowship, we experience a healthy blend of vertical and horizontal engagement.

Notice the relational flow expressed in Psalm 34:3 (NKJV): *"Oh, magnify the Lord with me and let us exalt His name together."* We move from singular (me) to plural (us) to Divine (His), then land again on the all-inclusive (together). Though we are by nature relationally inconsistent, God has provided that HE will be the thread that stitches us together.

It is by Him that we are unified, then drawn as one into His presence through worship.

As His body, we are always dealing with the imperfections of one another, and at the same time, standing in the presence of the Only One Who Has No Imperfections.

Musically Excellent

Finally, we are commanded to be musically excellent as we shout to the Lord with joy (Psalm 33:3). Our ever-developing skills in worship set us free from the distractions of stage fright and performance anxieties. Instead of being stuck *"in the chart,"* eyes cast downward, we'll be soaring to ever higher heights of worship, our hearts, hands, and voices trained to work together as one.

Yes, we are very excited to set new goals and venture ahead with this First Light Worship Ministry mission statement. Worship hopes and worship dreams are emerging as we embrace the Lord's collective heart for our team.

My prayer is that you too will find His way, in your own words, to express the mission He has for you. He's created us to stand in His strength, bask together in His presence, and offer Him the very best that we have. A fresh mission and a clear team direction will help us to do just that. Now who are you, and what are you doing, all for the glory of God?

Love, Lift, and Lead (Applying Worship Team "Die-namics")

Love one another. Lift up praises as friends and bandmates. Lead others to join in as you worship the Lord together. Applying these three—loving, lifting, and leading—will create a firm foundation for a healthy, effective worship team—*yours!*

Skilled musicianship, exercised within the parameters of Biblical principles (loving one another as Christ loved and gave Himself for us) results in positive worship team function. When good musicians come together and defer to one another with the love of Christ, yielding their collective talents to lift up praises to God, great results can abound! Pretty soon, all those within earshot of your team are worshiping too, because you are loving, lifting, and leading!

Ephesians 2:10 (NKJV) says: *"We are His workmanship, created in Christ Jesus for good works, which God prepared beforehand that we should walk in them."*

As worshipers, this is the stuff our dreams are made of: great "worship exploits" (works) in the name of Jesus. Is there even one of us who doesn't keep this goal at the very core of his or her worship heart? We all desire to see the kind of fruit that comes from great "worship works"!

> In the absence of death to self, we have no worship life to offer anyone else!

But unless the seed (talent) falls to the ground and dies to itself first, it can never grow upward into the lofty paragon of praise it was created to be.

Team "Die-namics"

In the absence of death to self, we have no worship life to offer anyone else! As Philippians 2:3, 4 (NKJV) says: *"Let nothing be done through selfish ambition or conceit, but in lowliness of mind let each esteem others better than himself. Let each of you look out not only for his own interests, but also for the interests of others."*

Team *die-namics*—that is, each member of the team dying to self in order to serve others—is the pivotal point around which successful worship team ministry revolves. As long as we musicians are convinced of our own over-importance, singular calling, or talent that exceeds or supersedes that of anyone else, we will never love, lift, and lead together successfully. It is vital that we release our destructive ideas, attitudes, egos, and ambitions in favor of servanthood, submission, and self-awareness. We *must* be honest with ourselves about our own talent—or lack thereof, even if Mama (bless her heart) always told us how wonderful we were!

Love

Mates. Buds. Friends. Brothers and sisters. Joint heirs. Co-laborers. Spiritual *kinfolk* (if you're from the South). The list of words to describe our relational interconnectivity with those on our worship teams goes on and on. And these monikers carry great weight. They confer shared identity and value to participating team members, when of course the members are already bound together with that *secret ingredient* most commonly found in high-functioning teams: L-O-V-E.

Without love, we may end up calling each other every name in the book, but they certainly won't be the names that bind us together as a team! As I Corinthians 13 so perfectly puts it: *". . . the greatest of these is love."* Without it, our worship teams literally become as a *"sounding brass or a clanging cymbal."* Both brass and cymbals can certainly be used appropriately on a worship team, but are hardly substitutes for the "Super Glue of the heart": love. Love is what motivates us to die to ourselves in order to serve and submit to the needs and interests of others on our team.

Lift

OK. Let's assume that your worship team members love one another profusely! You're already dead to yourselves and totally serving one another and God in the spirit of unity and peace. Fantastic! Now let's practice together, with all our might, what we desire to do best: lifting up praises to Him.

I Chronicles 13:8 (NKJV): *"Then David and all Israel played music before God with all their might, with singing, on harps, on stringed instruments, on tambourines, on cymbals, and with trumpets."*

Let's do what David did, shall we? In the Old Testament, if you were going to war, you made music. If you were sad, you made music. If you were celebrating, you made more music. Dancing? Music. Worshiping? Music. Lamenting, repenting, presenting? Music, music, music! And as a result, guess what they became really good at? As they sang and played in a lifestyle way, they literally became the 288 skilled musicians spoken of in I Chronicles 25:7. They were the instrumentalists and singers who *"sounded as one"* in II Chronicles 5:13 and the singers who went out before the army in II Chronicles 20:21. (Just FYI: the singers won!)

When we spend plenty of time lifting up praises as a team, we're better prepared to deal with the unexpected distractions that inevitably happen in worship: buzzing cables, screaming babies, feedback, broken strings (or for that matter, broken hearts). We may never be called upon to go out before an army and sing, *"Praise the Lord, for His mercy endures forever,"* but the more we lift up His praises together as a team, the better prepared we'll be to respond with a resounding "Yes, Lord" to any worship situation He calls us to.

Hang out together. *Jam.* Improvise. Concertize. Write new songs. Rearrange old ones. Eat pizza, then sing around the table. Attend conferences and workshops. Listen to new tunes together and critique. Do just about anything you can to build friendships and musical partnerships with other team members. Travel together. Get comfy (like an old pair of favorite slippers on a cold winter's night). And if it gets too cold for ice cream, you can always eat pizza again! In other words, do everything you can to practice lifting up praises together in every situation. The more you experience together, the tighter the team becomes!

. . . And Lead

Psalm 22:22 (NKJV): *"I will declare Your name to my brethren; in the midst of the congregation I will praise You."*

We've determined to die to ourselves in order that we might manifest His love to one another as we practice lifting up His praises together. Sounds like a perfect plan, and with all of our might we will pursue it! Only one step left: *spread the worship bug.* Sneeze it. Cough it. Drool it if you have to. But lead it by always encouraging others to join you in the process. Whatever it takes to infect the entire world with an insatiable desire to honor God—do it! Loving, lifting, and leading are three extremely powerful elements in true worship team die-namics! Spread the bug! (I mean, Word).

What's the Use?
(Seven Ways to Offer Praise)

You might just need a larger worship team, or perhaps a smaller one will do. I guess it all depends upon whether you follow the Levitical example of worship in II Chronicles 5, or the Pauline expression in Acts 16. Either way, the Scriptures are brimming with hair-raising, fruit-bearing ways to offer praise. Our 21st-century challenge is not to contrive some edgy way to honor God. There's plenty of that already in the Bible. We have only to scan the Scriptures for their example, and step out in faith, trusting the Holy Spirit to appropriately direct our worship expression for the worship needs of the moment.

From and To

From Genesis to Revelation, worship commands a position of Biblical importance and priority. Perhaps no other thread, except for the redeeming work of Christ, ties the Scriptures together from end to end so well as worship. When tongues have ceased, knowledge has passed away, apostles, prophets, evangelists, pastors, and teachers are no longer needed, worship will continue, a never-ending homage to the One who alone is worthy to receive it.

So What's the Use?

When we keep our hearts open to Him, God never leaves us uninstructed or uninspired! Let's have a look at seven very practical ways our teams can practice praise in order to glorify the Lord. In a broad, general sense, these tips represent the myriad expressions of worship found in the Scriptures. They are intended for our application. Let's practice each one every day until they become an integral part of our daily worship lives.

1. Minister

As ministers, we need to be where the needs are. In I Chronicles 6:31, 32a, we find the Levites doing just that. They hung out in proximity to the worshipers. *"Now these are the men whom David appointed over the service of song in the house of the Lord, after the ark came to rest. They were ministering with music before the dwelling place of the tabernacle of meeting . . ."* (NKJV). What images does the word "ministering" bring to your mind? Lives being changed in a radical way? People healed, restored, and embraced? The Scripture says the Levites "ministered in the gates of the camp of the Lord." As a worship leader for many years, I've always imagined myself in that capacity: hanging out at the gates of the Lord's camp, listening to the Spirit for worship direction, identifying the needs of the people as they pass through, then targeting their needs appropriately with powerful praise and sensitive worship. Applied with heart surgery–like precision, our worship ministry can absolutely impact lives—forever!

2. Prophesy

I Chronicles 25:1a (NKJV) says: *"Moreover David and the captains of the army separated for the service some of the sons of Asaph, of Heman, and of Jeduthun who should prophesy with harps, stringed instruments, and cymbals . . ."* Two-hundred and eighty-eight worship musicians, all instructed in the songs of the Lord and skilled at their craft, is a worship leader's dream! And yet, this passage takes us far beyond musicianship or education and on to the marriage of spiritual gifting and skillfully executed playing: they prophesied with their instruments. They were instructed, by the king himself, to serve the Lord and the people by making music that was spiritually connected. Their inspired improvisation set the stage for the hearts of the people to be turned to worshiping God. *Improvisation by inspiration* equals playing prophetically. Be inspired to improvise.

3. Invite

In II Chronicles 5:12-14 (NKJV), we see the trumpeters (120 of them) and singers coming together as one, *"to make one sound to be heard in praising and thanking the Lord . . ."* This is an awesome passage to quote when dealing with those who think your worship music is too loud: *"one hundred and twenty priests sounding trumpets!"* Can you imagine the volume? Good thing they didn't have OSHA or decibel meters back then! But the powerful practical point of this passage is this: when God's people praise and worship Him in unity (including having a musically tight worship team), His presence can be sensed, often palpably. This passage goes on to say that *". . . the house of the Lord was filled with a cloud, so that the priests could not continue ministering because of the cloud; for the glory of the Lord filled the house of God"* (NKJV). Suddenly, all that hard work at rehearsals became quite worthwhile when the Levitical team and the people of God converged in one wonderful moment of jaw-dropping, eye-popping spiritual togetherness. When we invite the Lord's presence through our unity, He is faithful to show up!

4. Evangelize

Ever been thrown in jail? Didn't it just put you in the mood to sing happy songs? That is exactly what Paul and Silas did in Acts 16:25-34, and it caused an earthquake, a near suicide, and brought about the salvation of their jailer and his entire family. Odd how we sometimes limit God because of our lack of imagination or our overactive inhibitions. Even in the worst of circumstances, praising God is our best response. You never know who besides the Lord might be listening! It is always OK to obey the urge to praise.

5. Teach

"Let the word of Christ dwell in you richly in all wisdom, teaching and admonishing one another in psalms and hymns and spiritual songs, singing with grace in your hearts to the Lord." Colossians 3:16 (NKJV). Do you remember the ease of learning verse after verse of Scripture when you sang them instead of just memorizing by spoken repetition? I recall in the Youth with a Mission Leadership Training School that we were given one long passage of Scripture to memorize each week for twelve weeks. Right away, I began to write simple songs with each one and sing them over and over. When we were tested, I simply repeated the songs in my head as I wrote them out. Guess what: straight A-pluses! Sing the Scriptures and you won't forget 'em!

6. Bear Spiritual Fruit

Hebrews 13:15 (NKJV) says that *". . . the sacrifice of praise to God . . . is the fruit of our lips giving thanks to His name."* I Thessalonians 5:18 tells us to *"give thanks in everything."* How wonderful it is that our Heavenly Father considers thanking Him to be the sacrifice of (our) praise and the fruit of our lips. A grateful heart opens the door to deeper fellowship with Him. Praises from the lips begin with thanksgiving in the heart.

7. Praise God Forever!

OK, admittedly this one's a bit out of our reach for now, but someday our teams will join the *"great multitude which no one [can] number"* in crying out with a loud voice, *"Salvation belongs to our God who sits on the throne, and to the Lamb!"* Revelation 7:9, 10 (NKJV). What a privilege to carry in our hearts the knowledge that we are part of that never-ending stream of praises to our God: "Holy, holy, holy . . ." Eventually, people from every ethnos will enter into eternal exaltation.

The Use?

What's the use? We've only scratched the surface with ministering, prophesying, inviting, evangelizing, teaching, bearing spiritual fruit, and praising God forever. There are hundreds, maybe thousands, more uses of music and worship in the Scriptures. Until *that day*, let's do all we can to bring Him glory through a life that's lived in praise!

3

Worship Warm
(by Spending Time with God and Maintaining Musical Discipline)

Removing Distractions to the Worshiper's Heart

The essence of excellence is the absence of distraction!

Distractions come in many forms, from broken strings to broken hearts. Through these, our limited attention span is easily drawn away from the singular object of our affection during worship: Jesus Christ. When we remove distractions from worship, what's left are the things that truly edify and draw the listener/worshiper toward the heart of God. This is excellence in worship!

I Chronicles 25:6 talks about all those who were under the direction of their father for the music in the house of the Lord. They played cymbals, stringed instruments, and harps for the service in the house of God. Verse 7 points out that there were 288 of them who were instructed and skillful. Wow! What a stellar worship team they must have been! Excellent. I bet when they played, the congregation wasn't busy picking out all their bleeps and blunders. Instead, the people were free to keep their focus where it belonged: on the heart of God!

Pleasure

Probably the most important question related to worship excellence is, "Why bother?" Doesn't Psalm 100 say to *"make a joyful noise unto the Lord?"* That doesn't sound very excellent, does it? If it's OK to make a *noise* to the Lord, then why be musically proficient? What's our motivation? What drives us to the highest heights of worship skill development? Sadly, for many of us the answer has its roots in our own ego and insecurities. God forbid someone hear us blow it on our *axe!* So we practice, practice, practice until there's not the slightest possibility of a slip-up on stage. Then comes the attitude. We start to think that when the bright lights are shining on us, we'd better sound great and look even better! Whew! What a nasty way to approach an everlasting God! What we really need is a *Beatitude attitude: "blessed are the meek"*! This should be the reason we work so hard to become excellent. James 4:10 (NKJV) brings us loving correction: *"Humble yourselves in the sight of the Lord,"* it says, *"and He will lift you up."* It's His business whether anyone notices you, but your business to make sure that *everyone* notices Him!

There's only one reason to hone our worship skills to the most attainable point of perfection. When we're playing or singing at our very best, it's quite likely that we're not distracting others from their focus on God. We don't play for the pleasure of being noticed. Instead, we offer our best to God, removing potential mistakes that could become a real distraction to others!

Pressure

In contrast to the pleasure of the spotlight, there is also the pressure of fear, which can be a huge motivator to those of us driven to perfection! Here we stand in the spotlight again, but this time, instead of "struttin' our stuff 'cause we're so pumped up," quite the opposite is true. We become like deer in the headlights, frozen with anxiety. We experience a type of performance paralysis. Under those circumstances, nothing we could possibly play or sing would sound good to us. No lying mirror on earth could ever convince us that we're lookin' good now! The peril of performance pressure has prevailed. We have caved in. Our ship of praise has sailed. Whirling in a storm of self-doubt, we're smashed upon the rocks of distraction.

Here again is a great reason to strive for excellence. A high skill level brings with it confidence, and when we're confident, we are much less likely to fall prey to wrong notes, bad rhythms, and poor execution brought on by nervousness and anxiety.

The Big Finish

God's will is that we should not be slaves to the pleasure of the spotlight, or the pressure (fear) of performance! Neither brings any promise of worship excellence. Whether deceived by our own artificially inflated abilities or petrified at the mere thought of standing before people and ministering, we are the ones who create our own worship distractions. Thank God that He has given us the authority in Christ not to live under this kind of bondage!

Let's also remember that those who choose to follow us are directly affected by *our* distractions. As lead worshipers, one of our highest goals should be to break the chains of pleasure and pressure that so often hinder us in our genuine expressions to God. From this day forward, let's commit together to offer glorious praises to Jesus; distracted only by the power of His Divine presence to wing us to worship heights we've never flown before!

Heart, Hands, and Voices

Worshiping *warm* means spending time with God and maintaining musical discipline. Excellence follows preparation! Did you know that some of the best opera singers in the world rest their voices for as many as three days before a performance? Olympic athletes carefully stretch every muscle before they compete, reducing the risk of injury and increasing their chances for the gold.

The virtuoso violinist Nicolò Paganini often practiced scales and exercises for up to 15 hours a day! Fifteen!!

During his concerts Paganini was known to purposely break as many as three strings and play the rest of the piece on the one remaining! This bit of showmanship allowed him to demonstrate the incredible virtuosity that he earned at the high price of personal discipline. As worshipers, we too need to warm up. With regular, private offerings of heart, hands, and voices to the Lord, we are primed for powerful public praise. Our daily prayer should be, "Lord, get me out of the refrigerator of complacency and help me always to worship warm!"

Excellence follows preparation!

The Heart: Daily Devotion

One of the greatest examples of the daily life of the worshiper is found in Acts 2:42-47. It lists five habits of the early Church and the blessings that followed. By spending time in the Word, hanging out together, praying, giving, and witnessing, the first-century worshipers experienced the kind of life-changing results we also desire today. They spent time with God, and verse 47 (NKJV) says that as *"they were praising [Him]"* they enjoyed *"favor with all the people. And the Lord added to the church daily those who were being saved."* We can expect to see this same spiritual fruit in our lives as we practice the worship lifestyle of daily devotion demonstrated by those early Christians.

The Hands: Instrumental Engagement

Once we've established that our first priority is to have our hearts devoted to the Lord, we can begin to examine the more physical aspects of worshiping warm. Take a look at your hands. They can be placed over your heart in allegiance, "put to the plow," used to change a tire, burp a baby, scratch your head, or sign your name. What a marvelous, versatile creation! We often think of the voice as the instrument of the Spirit, but in I Chronicles 25:1 we find the musicians prophesying with *"harps, stringed instruments, and cymbals."* They were skillful with their hands. They practiced. They worshiped warm!

We may not have 15 hours a day to spend like Paganini did, but every minute we invest in raising our skill level brings greater ease and flow to our corporate worship times.

Minding the *Modes*

To warm up your hands, I suggest a simple modal exercise at the beginning of each practice session.

First, play a basic C major (*Ionian*) scale:

C - D - E - F - G - A - B - C

Next, begin on the second *scale degree*, D, and play:

D - E - F - G - A - B - C - D

This is known as D *Dorian*. Beginning on the third scale degree in the key of C is E *Phrygian*. Sound like Greek to you? That's because each of the seven modes is known by a Greek name. Now play:

E - F - G - A - B - C - D - E

Do you see the pattern? How about playing F *Lydian*? It begins and ends on the note F:

F - G - A - B - C - D - E - F

G *Mixolydian* begins and ends with G:

G - A - B - C - D - E - F - G

Now here's A *Aeolian*:

A - B - C - D - E - F - G - A

And finally, B *Locrian*:

B - C - D - E - F - G - A - B

Have you mastered the modes in the key of C? Perhaps now you'd like to try them in *every* key. Simply begin with any note in any key, build a major scale from it (Ionian mode), then continue to build Dorian, Phrygian, Lydian, Mixolydian, Aeolian, and Locrian modes upon the remaining scale degrees just as we did in the key of C.

Your hands will certainly be warmed up after you spend some time playing ascending and descending scales in each of the seven modes.

The Voice: Vocal Vitality

Given the example of world-class opera singers, perhaps getting enough sleep is the most effective way to ensure great worship vocals. Nothing restores the vitality of the voice like rest, rest, and more rest.

It's also important for singers to watch what they eat! Uh-oh! That's a tough one, considering it means no chocolate, no dairy, and (this is extremely painful) no caffeine before singing! Chocolate and dairy products coat the throat and restrict vibration. Caffeine dehydrates the vocal cords. It's best to go without for up to 24 hours before singing. (Now we understand why opera singers seem so sleepy!)

To prevent injury to the vocal cords, we should never clear our throats. The experts say, "simply swallow instead." (Did I just hear you clear?)

Sit or stand as tall as possible when you sing. Back straight, top of the head held high. The large pipes of the pipe organ play the low notes. The small pipes play the high notes. Our voices work in much the same way. Never lower your chin to reach down for those notes "in the basement." The longer the pipe, the lower the note. We should also be sure to wear loose clothing when we sing. Constrictive attire impedes the expansion and contraction of the *diaphragm*. To worship warm, we must be able to breathe freely.

Before discussing the vocal routine, let's consider the lilies of the field: they neither toil nor spin; but they sure do make many of us sneeze! Allergies can be seasonal or perpetual. As worship team members, we must be mindful of those who wheeze, sneeze, cough, or completely clam up because of perfume, cologne, aftershave, and yes, those beautiful Easter lilies. For some, it's almost impossible to sing after just one whiff.

Vocal Routine

When I served the local church behind "The Redwood Curtain" in Humboldt County, California, we enjoyed three services each Sunday morning. Even though we called them "mild, medium, and hot," the fact is, the singers had to be ready to worship warm from the first service to the last. Exciting growth in attendance in many churches has necessitated multiple services. This requires worship singers to develop sensible habits that protect their voices from strain and pain! Here are just a few suggestions that have proven to be quite effective:

1. Hit the ground humming. As soon as you rise, begin to wander around the house humming comfortable low notes, which slowly warm up the vocal cords. This exercise is particularly popular with the rest of my family, who are still snug in their beds before sunrise on Sunday mornings!
2. Vocalize with a warm-up CD during your drive to church.
3. Use a singer's throat spray to coat and soothe the throat between services. (Caution: Some sprays contain as much as 70 percent grain alcohol. We jokingly call these "the joy of the Lord in a bottle" or "Aunt Bee's Buzz!")

4. Drink lots of room-temperature water. (Avoid those Sunday morning doughnuts and—you guessed it—coffee!)

5. Sip herbal tea (caffeine free). There are special teas on the market that coat the throat and help to eliminate problems from oversinging. (At the same time, they claim to reduce your cholesterol, increase your antioxidant levels, and extend your lifespan by no less than 7.3 years! Better check the label on that . . .)

Heart, Hands, and Voices

There's an old Thanksgiving hymn that says, "Now thank we all our God with heart and hands and voices . . ." We can see from these lyrics that the wisdom of the ages didn't change! Good worship sense has always dictated that we worship warm, yielding our hearts, hands, and voices as offerings to the Lord. With just a few good worship habits, we can remain always ready to worship Him and lead others to do the same. *Worship warm!*

Part II

TIME TO TIGHTEN THE TEAM

4

Get Out of the Garage (Remembering "Less Is More")

In the Beginning

"Mommy, where do little worship teams come from?" "Good question, Tommy." From Jubal? The Levites? David? Paul? We know that God doesn't simply speak them into existence. There are steps to be taken; steps of faith that lead to fruit. Like any other functioning unit, a worship team must begin with a leader, a true leader. One who is strong, confident, visionary, pastoral, and . . . wait a minute: human!

Though it's been years, it seems like no time ago that I began serving as a Minister of Worship Arts in Santa Fe, New Mexico. The first thing I did? I stood before my new congregation and confidently suggested that in II Samuel Chapter 6, David was leaping and whirling in his underwear! Great first impression. Glad I didn't mention the part about Michal, David's wife, who had no more children after she criticized his uninhibited worship style!

Now that I'd made such a powerful first impression, I could proceed to build the new worship team, warts and all. No place left to go but up!

Free Formation

The first meaning of "team" according to *Webster's* is "two or more horses, oxen, etc., harnessed to the same plow." Team members subordinate their individual interests and opinions to the unity and efficiency of the group. Where do little worship teams come from? How do we find members, and develop these horses and oxen into a well-honed worship unit? The following are helpful suggestions for the lead worshiper (the responsible party) who's just forming a team. The goal is that the team will be your friends, co-laborers, and partners in ministry for years to come.

> *The world functions in a system of authority and subordination. In the body of Christ, we are about making friends, discipling, and mentoring in order to release people to bear fruit for the Kingdom.*

Determine

Determine? That sure sounds sterile, but all it really means is "find out whom you have to work with." In order to develop a leader's vision for your new team, you must determine the availability and musicianship level of potential members. Plan a special formation meeting and begin to get to know your new worship teammates. Relationship building should be one of your highest priorities. Determine who best fits your vision and pursue them.

Hold Auditions

Ouch! "You mean the worship leader has to hear me play or sing by myself?" The audition is as much a relationship builder as it is an opportunity to hear and place team members where their gifts are most beneficial. Use this time as an opportunity to establish trust between the leader and follower. Blessed are the meek . . . on both sides of the leader/follower hierarchy.

Build Relationships

Not only do we need to know the musicianship level of team members, we need to understand their spiritual lives as well. Spend lots of time with your team outside of rehearsals. Create an online group and stay in touch. Have one-on-one coffee meetings. Eat meals together. Watch movies (instructional, spiritual, and entertaining). Minister together outside the four walls! Take mission trips together. Attend worship and Christian music conferences as a team. The world functions in a system of authority and subordination. In the body of Christ, we are about making friends, discipling, and mentoring in order to release people to bear fruit for the Kingdom.

> *Discuss issues ranging from dress codes to Greek modes.*

Disciple Your Team

The absence of growth equals death. Spend time identifying and addressing discipleship needs within the team. Create handouts that discuss issues ranging from dress codes to Greek modes. At the beginning of each rehearsal, have prayer and teaching time (keep these periods short). Sponsor churchwide, even community-wide, worship workshops. Enjoy special times of worship and ministry as a team. It's vitally important for us each to have our spiritual batteries recharged!

Create Together

The best way for team members to get on the same page and take personal ownership of the team vision is to create that vision together. Spend plenty of time in prayer, worship, and brainstorming as you write down what the Holy Spirit is saying to each heart. Next, create a mission statement that clearly and concisely articulates the heart of the team for God and God's specific calling for the team. You'll never again have to wonder whether you're worshiping in the right direction. Just as Abraham Lincoln did, share your vision, repeat your vision, then share your vision again. Keep it in front of the team members, elders, deacons, pastors, and everyone you're leading. Never let anyone forget who you are, and what you're about in worship! When it's time for your team to lead, you'll experience a unified focus, resulting in a powerful response.

Skills to Fill the Bill
(Identify, Develop, and Deploy)

I'm amazed. I didn't really see it coming. I think I was looking for it all along—sort of—but somehow it just snuck up on me. Now that it's here, I'm blown away! I want to shout it from the rooftops: "My worship team has skill!" That's right: S-K-I-L-L! I recognize their *intuitive flow*, polished performance, and teamwork. Their improved skill levels have resulted in a heightened worship experience for all involved. That seemingly ragtag bunch of individuals I began to work with over five years ago has actually become a band! They now have the skills to fill the bill! (Can you tell I'm excited?!)

Identify

It's very cool how people will step up to the plate if you just put a bat in their hands and shout, "Swing!" But as a worship leader, far too often I have underestimated the skill potential of those I'm leading. Many people have a tremendous amount of talent—it just needs to be identified. All an aspiring talent really needs is someone they respect to say, "Go for it. Swing that bat!" A little nudge, and soon they're hitting home runs. If we fail to identify their talent, they may never take that plunge into the deeper waters of skill development. Let's always be on the lookout . . .

Develop

1. Factor in Solitude

Now that we've identified potential, the individual must spend some serious alone time developing and polishing those fledgling skills. They must soak in solitude. Did you begin singing or playing music at an early age? Do you recall the story of the stereotypical parent (perhaps your own) screaming out the front door at little Johnny to stop whatever fun thing he's doing, and come inside to practice? The way my parents tell it, they encountered the opposite problem. Instead of insisting that I leave my buddies and come practice, they almost had to push me out the front door to force me to take a break from my hours of self-imposed musical education. I was driven! (Is that unusual?)

The fact is, driven isn't always bad! There's a point in every promising musician's life when he or she must participate in a *schloggfest*. A what? A schloggfest! That's where the rubber meets the road. It's that alone time when you really dig in to hone your skills and prepare to be used by God in glorifying His name for His Kingdom. Without that "schlogg time" of practice, practice, practice, it is doubtful whether anyone could really become proficient at their musical endeavor. Gotta pay your dues . . .

2. Encourage Intuitive Flow

OK. Let's say that each individual on the team is now highly skilled. They've all put in the necessary schlogg time to be ready to worship together. What's the next level the team should aspire to? May I suggest intuitive flow?

Intuitive flow is when the team begins to move seamlessly from one song to the next without any hiccups in between. We become so connected by the sheer volume of time we spend together playing and ministering that it's almost as if we're thinking with one mind. We flow in unity from one worship tune to another, or from one key to the next, and remove that awkward silence—those pregnant pauses—from the worship set. This allows those we're leading to remain focused as we *segue,* almost without their noticing, from glorious praise to glorious praise.

Developing that intuitive flow requires spending lots of time together. We can achieve it by linking worship songs with *intervals* of personal or corporate expression. One way to facilitate this link is to use *free worship chord progressions*. These progressions are a repeatable sequence of chords that can be tagged onto the end of a praise or worship song and played again and again until the leader signals it's time to move on. As we become more comfortable with the intuitive flow of seamless worship, our corporate worship times will no longer resemble stop-and-go traffic on a busy thoroughfare. Instead, the bumps in the road to worship will disappear as we seamlessly glide up the highway toward Heaven. Why not "get your motor runnin' and head out on the highway," beginning to practice free worship chord progressions with your team? Spend some time between songs playing repeatable chord progressions until they become intuitive and second nature. (See Chapter 7: Find the Flow for free worship chord progressions.)

3. Polish Your Performance

Now back to the solitude of personal practice. *Licks* are the result of learned scales, modes, and *arpeggios*. They take some precious personal practice time, but when applied in a team setting, they give our performance a sense of polish! Need to solo? Inspired to improvise by the Holy Spirit? Put some licks and tricks in your musical tool box, and you'll find you're ready when the moment is yours.

Deploy

". . . *indeed it came to pass, when the trumpeters and singers were as one, to make one sound to be heard in praising and thanking the Lord, and when they lifted up their voice with the trumpets and cymbals and instruments of music, and praised the Lord, saying: 'For He is good, for His mercy endures forever,' that the house, the house of the Lord, was filled with a cloud . . .*" II Chronicles 5:13 (NKJV).

Nothing seems to feel better to the worship musician than the sense that everyone on the team is pulling together to honor God. There is unity. And when we practice unified praise, as was done by the Levites in II Chronicles, we can expect to enjoy the exceptional results that they did. We will see the glory of the Lord fill His house. And we are not just limited to the four walls of a church building. We already have Christ in us!

I've set a goal this year. Now that my team is displaying intuition, polish, and teamwork, I believe it's time to deploy. Oh, they've already been out there week after week at the local church level, but what about taking it to the streets? Is there any reason why a well-honed worship team can't represent at open mike nights, community events, public prayer times, festivals, or arts and crafts shows? There are flea markets, rodeos, and fiestas galore in my home town. I'm sure your community hosts lots of similar events. These are splendid opportunities to go out and be an example of what it means to have the skills to fill the bill! And remember, while you're out there ministering together, your team will just get better and better! It's a win-win proposition. Others hear the Word and respond in worship, and you grow together in skills that will ultimately glorify the One who created them in the first place. Ready to go for it?

Get Out of the Garage

Not long ago I found myself sitting at a four-way stop intersection. It was a sunny day, and the windows were down. I heard noise—incessant noise— freight-train-level noise! I glanced across the intersection, and just a bit to the left. That's when I spotted them. They were in a garage. Flailing, screaming, and writhing, they exploded with high energy. No, the place wasn't on fire, it was just your garden-variety *garage band* doing what garage bands do. They were young and full of passion, every voice and instrument singing and playing simultaneously at full volume.

There's a lot to be said for that type of exuberance. There's also a lot to be said for poison oak as relates to flailing, writhing, and screaming. The question is, does that level of reckless expression work in the worship context? In Psalm 33:3b (NKJV) we are commanded to *"play skillfully with a shout of joy."* In order to do so we must live the worship lifestyle through team mission based on Biblical principles. We also need to worship warm by spending time with God and maintaining musical discipline. Unlike the tsunami of sound emanating from that garage, our music should breathe and allow us to feel the dynamic rise and fall of worship. We must get out of that garage with poise and polish! But how?

> *The rule is "one eye on the Lord and one eye on the leader." Unless you're an alien with three eyes, this rule doesn't leave much opportunity to focus on self!*

A Quick Review

Let's open the garage door with a quick review of some of the band basics used by professionals. Knowing your own voice or instrument is of primary importance. We need to practice phrasing, tone, chord voicings, scales, modes, licks, and tricks. It's vital to spend time at home perfecting our personal musical skills. Once we've mastered the basics we can begin to follow the leader and get our eyes off ourselves. We need to be able to watch for hand signals and other cues. The rule is *"one eye on the Lord and one eye on the leader."* Unless you're an alien with three eyes, this rule doesn't leave much opportunity to focus on self!

Be sure to check the *key signature,* and watch out for *chromatics.* Nothing says *train wreck* like a sharp and a natural accidentally playing at the same time! Once we've established the key, we're free to move upward together with key changes or *modulations* (see Chapter 8: Make the Mod). Our expressions of worship should always flow in an upward direction.

Get Out!

Now let's put it in gear and get out on the road. The following three suggestions are guaranteed to help move your team from the garage to the super-highway in under 60 seconds flat! (Maybe.)

I remember a little beginner guitar called the *Stella.* It was an armored tank of a guitar, small and virtually indestructible. What it lacked in tone and playability it made up for in sheer endurance. But as much as I loved that little six-string wonder, there's no way I'd use it now in a progressive, professional setting. The goal for worship team members is to use the highest-quality gear possible. It's amazing what an upgrade in instruments, amps, and sound reinforcement will do for your professionalism!

After we've acquired the best equipment, it's a great idea to have a regular maintenance schedule. Change those batteries and strings. Set the intonation on your guitar. Tune the acoustic piano. Buy new drum sticks and guitar picks. Attention to maintenance helps to create a worship environment without distractions.

Another *must do* is to use an electronic tuner for all tunable instruments. This brings consistency to our sound and removes a potentially huge distraction to worship: *praise twang.*

Don't forget that less is more! There are two elements that make up music: notes and rests. The rests are just as important as the notes! It's OK for some to rest while others play. *"Let each of you regard one another as more important than himself."* Philippians 2:3b (NKJV). What that means in the worship setting is to leave holes for improvisational prophetic expression by inspiration (see I Chronicles 25:1, 6, 7). In other words, no *lick hogs!*

Instrument Arrangements

Ready to cruise? One of the most efficient ways to keep our bands out of the garage is to use clean, uncluttered instrument arrangements. When we master this, we're ready to make a run for the finish line! The rule is really quite simple: the more band members we have on the team, the less each one needs to play.

Two Guitars

Suppose we're using an electric guitar and an acoustic guitar. The acoustic guitar rhythmically strums or fingerpicks while the electric guitar plays fills, licks, and leads. If there are two acoustic guitars on the team, one should strum chords in the first position (first four frets) while the other does alternate chord voicings up the neck, or even uses a *capo*. The idea is to spread out the sound so that each instrument has its own niche. Imagine how that would sound if it were recorded and mixed in stereo: one guitar in the left speaker and one in the right speaker. Now you get my drift.

Two Keyboards

With two keyboards, we apply the same spatial principle. One plays piano-style arpeggios, fills, and chords, while the other plays *pads* (strings, organ, or other *legato* parts). Remember, keyboardists: when playing with a bass guitarist, try not to play too low or too heavily with the left hand. The bass guitar and the lower notes on the electronic keyboard share common frequencies. Playing them simultaneously can cause low-frequency rumble.

Drums and Percussion

When working with a drummer and percussionist, the drums cover the basic rhythm and some fills. The percussion instruments play the alternate rhythms, fills, and *syncopation*.

Bass Guitar and Kick Drum

A wonderful way to tighten up the team is to make sure that the bass guitar and kick drum are in sync. This generally means that they are both playing a strong first and third beat of each measure. Providing a solid rhythmic foundation for the team will raise its confidence level and help bring musical unity. This gives us the freedom to express our deep, heartfelt worship!

Going . . .

Now to get us going, let's parallel our teams with the analogy found in Ephesians 4:16 (NKJV). What's important is that we remember that we're part of *"the whole body* (worship team), *being fitted and held together by that which every joint* (voice or instrument) *supplies, according to the proper working of each individual part, [which] causes the growth of the body for the building up of itself in love."* This is how we get our team out of the garage and on the road to excellence. *Gone!*

What Could Possibly Go Wrong?
(Maintaining Technical Excellence)

Yesterday, it happened. Just about anything that could go wrong during worship did go wrong. The day started out predictably enough. That incredibly blue Santa Fe sky greeted me as I walked out the front door to head for the church. The engine of my fine old Ford fired right up, and soon the radio was blaring Dick Clark, espousing the glory of the Oldies Top 40. (For some Sunday-morning worship inspiration, I switched to the black gospel station as quickly as possible.)

Then What Went Wrong?

As always, we conducted our weekly worship team tech rehearsal on Thursday afternoon. That's the point in the week when we go through the worship checklist. From batteries to lyric projection, lighting, and stage setup, we try to make sure that everything is just right before the team shows up for Thursday evening rehearsal.

After ensuring that the charts were accurate and available for each worship song in the set, we welcomed the team members as they showed up for "P and P" (prayer and polish). The rehearsal proceeded without a glitch. This further compounded our Sunday morning dismay when we discovered that "worship gremlins" had been hard at work over the weekend.

It began during the very first song of the first service. Inexplicably, a middle-aged light bulb in one of our three video projectors croaked (we have since replaced the projectors with flat screens!). If you're like most worship leaders and team members, one of your high-priority goals is to minimize these types of distractions during worship. The instantaneous blackness of the screen, lit up only moments before with the morning's first glowing words of praise, jerked the attention of the worshipers from the eternally Divine back into the momentarily mundane. Sometimes it only takes one small stone to start an avalanche. The tumbling had begun!

Right on the heels of the video bulb debacle came the wireless mic muting mishap. So much damage can be caused by one stray index finger on a Mute button. That's all it took to accidentally render two perfectly new double A batteries useless. This was distraction number two, and it wasn't diagnosed until the end of the first service.

When our bass player arrived for service number two, he was greeted by the total re-tweaking of all the settings on his stage amp. Who changed it? Who knows? The gremlins we suppose, but suffice to say that he spent the rest of the morning trying to arrive back at that low-frequency sweet spot he had so carefully dialed in at rehearsal just three days before. Distraction number three was in full swing.

It was then that the gremlins launched their most insidious attack. As previously mentioned, it is our habit to check and replace batteries every Thursday for the following Sunday. This time, what we thought was a brand new 9-volt battery in the internal preamp of my Taylor T5 was actually a used one, lying in wait to disrupt worship with a final choke and wheeze of DC output. This turned my beautifully clear signal into a dynamically distorted distraction. "OK," I thought, "it's time for the people out there to meet and greet one another. I'll just discreetly change the battery while they're not looking." I signaled the sound tech to mute my guitar channel, and in seconds I had a brand new 9-volt battery in the T5. "Finally," I thought, "after a morning of multiple distractions, we are back on track, ready to lead the people into the throne room of God!"

Not so fast! Yet one more hurdle of distraction remained, and this was a good one. No sooner did we begin the next praise song than we noticed a hideous crackle and spit coming from my guitar channel. Arrggghh! The battery was fine now, but sometime during that short welcome break, the gremlins had made their final move. The *XLR cable* between the guitar *direct box* and *house snake* had chosen that moment to cease making a solid connection. For the next 20 minutes or so there were milliseconds at a time of pure clarity, interspersed with eardrum-wrenching electronic outbursts. My worship leader focus was gone. Demoralized, I grimaced through the remainder of the set, then slunk off the stage with my head hung low.

The Path of Prevention

We learned that day that not every worship distraction can be avoided. In spite of any technical challenges we may face, we must rely on the work of the Holy Spirit in the hearts of the people to overcome some distractions. I actually received one surprisingly wonderful praise report from someone who was deeply ministered to that morning. She never even noticed any of the worship distractions. There's a wonderful old saying: "You do your best and God will do the rest." There's probably no more appropriate context for that than during our worship times, and yet, as responsible lead worshipers, there are steps we should take on the path of prevention. Here are a few suggestions. They may not eliminate all of your technical challenges, but if applied, they will send your gremlins a clear message that you are on the offensive.

1. Regularly replace batteries, strings, bulbs, and anything else that has a short, unpredictable life span. This will help you avoid lots of embarrassment and distractions. Make and stick to a regular, consistent schedule of replacement.

2. Keep consistent records. Keeping a written log of your amp, instrument, and sound reinforcement settings will make it easy to reset them to your favorite sweet spots. Also, remember to keep an eye on how many hours any gear that has its own internal clock has been used. Too many hours can be a warning sign of impending problems. Stay vigilant.

3. Have supplies on hand. Always have extra fresh batteries, cables, bulbs, strings, picks, sticks, and anything else you can think of. You never know when you might need to make a quick switch right in the middle of a worship service. By diminishing the number of potential distractions during worship, we increase the level of focus on the One we came to honor in the first place.

4. Don't forget to pray! It's not weird to pray for your instruments, amps, sound system, computers, lights, projectors, or anything else that assists your team in offering the ultimate glory to God. Spend time in prayer with the team every chance you get. You'll never regret it.

5. Finally, *fluidity* is the key! I've often heard it said, "Be fluid, because flexible is

too rigid." These profound words of wisdom, applied to worship preparation and mixed with faith, will enable us to deal with anything that could possibly go *worng*—that is, wrong.

Who Else Can Be *Your* Very Best? (Maintaining Relational Excellence)

Frustrations are running rampant! The others on our worship team just don't seem to be living up to our standards of excellence. Week after week we spend Sunday afternoon analyzing their performance and wondering why they just didn't measure up. We must be trapped in some kind of worship-warp. It seems we've blasted off and landed on a forbidden planet where truth turns into opinion, direction into criticism, and forgiveness into "let's wait and see . . ." How do we escape from this alternate universe of comparisons? Why do we continue to measure everyone else by the standards we should be setting for ourselves? After all, who else can be *our* very best?

The Naked Truth

Please allow me to bare my soul! In the early 1990s, it was an extreme privilege to find myself teaching in a well-known international School of Music Ministry. Far more illustrious instructors than I had gone before me, and I was giddy with excitement to follow in their gigantic footsteps. It was humbling and frightening to join forces with those I considered to be Christian music icons, but we shared a common vision, and we were willing to go to great lengths to see others in every nation prepared and sent out in all directions to glorify God.

> *It was I who tumbled headlong into that bottomless pit of critical perfectionism!*

The experience began as you might expect: relationship building, playfully testing one another's abilities, and enjoying the freedom of worship-jamming with a highly skilled team of professionals. In light of such a stellar start, it's hard to believe how quickly the downward spiral of judgment and criticism set in. They weren't criticizing me—not that I know of. It was I who tumbled headlong into that bottomless pit of critical perfectionism! Sadly, it seems that I was applying a higher standard to others than I was to myself. You know, if you really work at it, you can dig yourself a BIG hole with a very small shovel!

The Even Nakeder Truth

The internalized criticism escalated. Soon I was miserable. My opinions started to overflow into worship times. I could no longer easily stand on the same stage with some of my co-worshipers. Their imperfections were just too glaring! The petty frictions mounted. One team member was never on time; another had no charts prepared. Yet another didn't even bring a guitar pick to rehearsal! What kind of professionalism was that? My scrutiny intensified. No detail was so small that I couldn't find something wrong with it. I began to think their timing was off. Pitches were out. *Tempos* were too fast or too slow. They complained. They were insecure. They were control freaks! They, they, they! Everyone on that team was in some way wrong. Everyone . . . but me.

> *The Lord knows we'd drown in an ocean of our own guilt if He were to show us our true insides in one big flash flood!*

The lightbulb moment had come. Everyone but *me*? I'm never wrong? Over time I had attached a negative trait, experience, or habit to every single relationship. Instead of the respect and (probably) submission the team members were due, they were getting nothing but walking papers from me. Dude! Why didn't I just look in the mirror?

I wish I could say that this revelation came in a profound sort of way. A parting-of-the-Red-Sea-type experience would have been in order. But often, life changes come in tiny sprinkles instead of torrential downpours. The Lord knows we'd drown in an ocean of our own guilt if He were to show us our true insides in one big flash flood! Gradually, though, the reality of my guts came into focus. Deep down I was addicted to criticism! The ability to see the best in others, as related in I Corinthians 13, had departed from me. My attitude was a spiritually lethal poison, killing off the calling and anointing of God in my life! (Note to self: Bless, and curse not!)

The Truth (for Real)

True worshipers spend a lot of time blessing God. We're learning, writing, practicing, and honing our skills, all to give Him greater glory. But if we find ourselves blessing God at the same time we're cursing our fellow worship team members, we are guilty of James 3:8-10 (NKJV), and have rendered our praises ineffective:

"But no man can tame the tongue. It is an unruly evil, full of deadly poison. With it we bless our God and Father (we stand in front of the congregation and worship our socks off) *and with it we curse men* (we badmouth and criticize our brothers and sisters who are standing on our right and left in worship partnership) *who have been made in the likeness of God. Out of the same mouth proceed blessing* (to God) *and cursing* (to man). *My brethren, these things ought not to be so."*

The truth is, no one but Jesus can live up to our expectations, and certainly no one else can be your very best but you. Even in a *super band* setting, there are multiple reasons for criticism and judgment. If we allow them, these negative feelings can undermine and destroy the very fabric of our worship ministry. How frightful to imagine ourselves standing before Jesus on the Last Day. He's shaking His head at the way we've squandered the indescribably powerful gifts of worship and music we've been given. We've wasted His time and ours on squabbling, criticizing, and complaining about those He specifically created to stand shoulder to shoulder with us for glory to Himself.

The motives, gifts, habits, and ideologies of others will never perfectly line up with our own. The truth is, we do our best team fishing (team building) in the catch-and-release zone. First, reel in others (catch them carefully through good relationship building). Once on shore, admire the awesome beauty and gifts of God in them. Finally (and this is a *biggie*), let them off the hook!

Just as the sport fisherman releases the fish back into the water to swim again, our final step requires that we release our partners back into ministry. We allow them to swim free of criticism and the weight of our unrealistic expectations. When we cease to bait our hooks with comparison and pride, we facilitate the uninhibited praise of others to the Almighty God.

Now we've broken free from the critical worship warp and are soaring with unified hearts into the very presence of our eternal Savior, Jesus Christ! It's true: no one else can be your very best. They shouldn't have to. That job is simply left to you!

Plus 10 for the Tight Team
(Just 10 Percent More Times 10!)

A worship time is like an iceberg. Most of what goes on in preparation for presentation is under the surface, out of the public view. The congregation rarely sees more than the tip. Behind the scenes (or under the water, as the case may be) there are a myriad of activities, attitudes, commitments, disciplines, and sacrifices that must be properly maintained and subjugated to the will of God. All these exist for one glorious purpose: to support our worship moments and make them extra special every time.

"Now to Him who is able to do exceedingly abundantly above all that we ask or think, according to the power that works in us, to Him be glory in the church by Christ Jesus . . ." Ephesians 3:20, 21a (NKJV).

What if I told you that even though your whole team is already giving 100 percent, you could still give that much more to the Lord through your worship ministry? Sound too good to be true? I know, I know—100 percent plus 100 percent equals 200 percent. But in God's economy, nothing is ever too far out to be considered. Remember, He's able to do, even in our weakness, *"exceedingly abundantly above all that we ask or think!"* The old adage applies: "One sure way not to reach our goals is never to make any!" We need to be making lofty worship plans, and exercising faith that He will bring them to pass, *"exceedingly abundantly above."* If we shoot for the stars, perhaps at least we'll reach the tops of the trees together. Ready to fly?

More than Your All

What does it mean to give more than your all? At first glance, it looks like either a daunting challenge, a trick question, or at best an oxymoron. We've all heard about how to eat an elephant: one bite at a time. The same bite-size principle works for pushing past our apparent earthly limitations in worship ministry. We don't have to add an extra 100 percent of effort in one pachyderm-sized chunk, either. Instead, as we sing, play, connect, praise, touch, minister, love, feel, and empathize with those we are leading, we begin to identify areas where we can give just a little bit more each time. I believe the sum total of each of the individual increases will quickly add up to that extra 100 percent we're hoping for!

Can you think of areas in your worship ministry that you've already contemplated improving or increasing a bit? How about the daily devotion and relationship of team members to the Lord? Could that area be ramped up 10 percent? On the horizontal plane, are the team members reaching out to one another in brotherly/sisterly support and encouragement on a regular basis? Are they also connecting with the congregation in a personal, ministerial sort of way? Turn that knob to the right 10 percent too. What about increasing our attention to personal disciplines? It's hard to consistently minister to the Lord and His people when our personal spiritual lives are not in good order. That's another 10 percent.

You can see that it won't be long until we've made the leap from zero to 100. In increments of just 10 percent times 10, we'll be giving 100 percent more than our all to the One who's worthy beyond all our imagination!

The Great Reminder

The first and greatest commandment says to love God above all else. The second is like it: love others as yourself. By default, we love ourselves last. We'll begin our journey on the path to 10 percent more times 10 by grouping our percentage-growth-priorities according to Matthew 22:37-40. Let's call it "the Great Reminder." I suggest creating your own list, prioritized with God at the top, others second, and yourself last. Base it on the personal and corporate worship needs of the body where you serve. The following are just a few examples to help you get started. After reflecting on these, take some time to consider and implement your own "Plus 10 for the Tight Team" goals. You'll be amazed at the changes.

God

Loving God comes first. Since we can be so easily distracted, why not begin by adding 10 percent more focused energy to every worship-related activity we do, especially our worship times?

Another way to express our love for God, and keep Him first in our thoughts, is to focus the lyrics of our songs in His direction. Many of today's praise and worship tunes have "I" or "me" at the center. Though this can help to boost the effectiveness of horizontal ministry, may I also suggest that we add 10 percent more tunes to our worship sets that dwell solely on the divine attributes of God, our Creator and Savior? Why not purpose our words to pour out in praises aimed directly at God? Let's use 10 percent more pronouns like "You" and "He" in place of "I" and "me."

Others

Next, we should explore some ways to increase our loving and relating to others through our worship. Let's increase our team rehearsal and technical preparation time by 10 percent. Perhaps even add a special vocal rehearsal or create a "make sure" list for the technical team to check each week.

What if we also spent just 10 percent more time in prayer together as a team? We could create a buddy system that facilitates praying for, mentoring, or discipling one another on a personal basis.

Not only within the team, but throughout the entire church, 10 percent more ministry to the people would certainly yield tremendous fruit!

And there's another area of potential increase that should never be overlooked: recreation! Why not pursue 10 percent more FUN with our teams? Nothing helps to solidify relationships like "hang time"—just doing what we enjoy together!

Self

Finally, some self-improvement in worship is in order. If we invested 10 percent more time in daily personal devotion (prayer, Bible study, worship time); 10 percent more time in daily study of worship books, DVDs, workshops, seminars, and websites; 10 percent more time in daily personal warmup (voices and instruments); and 10 percent more time in daily personal practice, we wouldn't even recognize our worship selves after about two weeks! Just imagine the growth potential and improvement on the corporate worship level if we were all to give appropriate attention to our individual worship-devotion habits.

As worship ministers, we should always be on the lookout for ways to bring increases of fruit and effectiveness to ministry. Today, I'm committing to 10 percent more prayer for *you*, that the Lord will reveal His specific growth goals for your life and worship ministry. May He always lead you down the path of ever-increasing returns—at least a 10 percent increase at a time!

5

Sing Like a Sandwich

Welcome to the Club

WARNING: Reading the following could make you ravenous. That's right—*ravenous*!

The key to strong, satisfying vocal harmonies is to *sing like a sandwich*. Yes, sir. Two delicious pieces of harmonic whole wheat with a luscious slab of Grade-A melodic roast beef in the middle. *Mmmm-mmmm*. Now that's the way to harmonize! [Insert snack here.]

To understand tight, contemporary vocal harmonies, let's visualize it this way: The beef represents the melody line, usually sung by the lead worshiper—the congregation— and doubled by one or more background vocalists.

The first harmony (whole-wheat slice #1) sits a third above the melody line (the beef) and is sung by those with a comfortably higher *pitch range*.

The second harmony (whole-wheat slice #2) also sits above the melody, this time by an interval of a fifth. But in order to create our three-part harmonic sandwich, we must drop the fifth an *octave*. This harmony is sung by those with a comfortably lower pitch range, and creates a *first inversion* of the triad. Now the notes are stacked: 5 (lower pitch range), 1 (melodic line), and 3 (higher pitch range). In this way we achieve the tight, contemporary effect we're aiming for. This is the secret recipe for a delightful vocal harmonic sandwich!

It's time to diversify into that harmonic cacophony of auditory delights known as three-part harmony.

But to Start With . . .

Sometimes it's just nice to have all the vocalists sing the melody line in unison first. That now-familiar saying, *less is more*, really applies here. If the BGVs (background vocals) are always singing harmony, we begin to take that wonderfully pleasing sound for granted. In order to add variety, let's work first on a unified vocal blend for our worship team. Breathy warm tones and phrasing should all rise and fall as one beautiful, heavenly sound. Properly blended, BGVs in unison can take the listeners to worship places they've never been before. Then, when that well-worked three-part harmony finally kicks in, *boom!* God can use it to inspire an even higher level of worship expression.

Remember what happened in II Chronicles 5:7-14? After what must have been a spectacular rehearsal, the Levites who were singers (they also played cymbals, stringed instruments, and harps) joined together with 120 priests sounding trumpets. The Scripture says that when they were as one, to make one sound to be heard in praising and thanking the Lord, that the house of the Lord was filled with a cloud. Then the glory of the Lord filled the house of God! I'm not sure I've seen it happen that way just lately, but isn't it one of the highest goals of the worship team to see God's glory revealed among and upon His people? The unity of their hearts, voices, and instruments invoked the palpable presence of God. Unison is a good thing!

Then What?

Once we've achieved an angelic blend of unified voices, it's time to diversify into that harmonic cacophony of auditory delights known as three-part harmony. Time for a sandwich! Here are a few things to consider before we dive headlong into that vast sea of harmonic vocal possibilities.

1. Verify Vocal Range

Many sweet-hearted worship singers with divinely inspired motives have no idea what their own vocal range is. It is imperative to establish this in order to properly place worship team singers within the ensemble. Here's the rule of thumb for determining who sings which notes.

Speaking from the sandwich paradigm, the melody singers (beef) generally have a range from C to C. This is the standard comfortable *tessitura* or pitch range for congregational singing. Since that's whom we're ultimately leading into worship, we must be ever mindful of the people in the pews.

Those represented by the upper whole-wheat slice are able to exceed the average congregational range and reach from C up an octave, continuing all the way to G.

Conversely, those represented by the lower whole-wheat slice will sing in a range that resides below the melodic line. Test for those with a range from F, up an octave, and continuing through D. Establishing the vocal range of the singers on your team will avoid lots of frustration, and not a few purple faces.

2. Practice Vocal Blend

Vocal blend happens in real time, adjusted moment by moment. It is vital that the worship team vocalists listen closely to one another, gauging their volume, pitch, and tone from note to note and section to section. The sound person can give them a head start by providing an evenly distributed monitor mix. The truer the monitor, the more easily the individual can adjust his or her volume to achieve optimum blend.

Exercises in dynamics during rehearsals also help to condition individuals to be honest with themselves concerning their true volume in the mix. The vocalists should spend some time standing in a circle and facing inward. Singing without microphones, they will be able to listen closely to their blend with one another. During subsequent worship times, this heightened awareness of natural blending will translate into a more professional, polished presentation.

3. Learn to Listen

Once we've established who is singing which part, and have arrived at a warm, pleasant vocal blend, it's time to train our ears to listen for the correct notes that define harmonic intervals. These should consistently reflect the intervallic movement of the lead vocal or melody line.

Learning to listen closely is probably the best way to maintain a harmonic interval relative to the melody line of a song. As a kid, I used to love to listen to the Everly Brothers. It was so very kind of them to sing in two-part harmony, and by default, invite me to join in with the third part. During my worship life, God has redeemed the harmonies in songs like "Wake Up Little Susie" and "All I Have to Do Is Dream" in order to bring glory to Himself. Listening closely really pays off!

A favorite worship song for helping background vocalists get comfortable with hearing and singing their harmony parts is "Come, Now Is the Time to Worship" by Brian Doerksen. For a nice variation, try singing three-part harmony during the chorus, then switch to unison vocals for the bridge. Other standards, like "Here I Am to Worship" by Tim Hughes, "You Are So Good to Me" (specifically the bridge) by Ben and Robin Pasley, and the chorus on "Hallelujah (Your Love Is Amazing)" by Brenton Brown lend themselves easily to harmonic instruction and implementation.

Chordal Ear Training

Finally, take some time with the team to develop a harmonic comfort zone, vocally moving from one familiar chord voicing to another. Beginning with an A *major chord*, have everyone sing and hold "La." Lower range sings E, melody sings A, and upper range sings C♯.

Now move from the A major chord to an A *minor chord* by having the upper-range voices drop their C♯ one *half step* to C.

After moving back up to A major, create an A2 chord by lowering the upper-range harmony note again, this time a *whole step* to B.

Try this same exercise using *IV chords*, *major 7ths*, *add 9s*, and so on. By practicing chordal movement, worship harmonizers will learn to sing their parts consistently above and below the melodic line.

This is singing like a sandwich. Now how 'bout some lunch?

6

Check the Chart
('Cause If You Don't Know Where You're Going . . .)

The Art of the Chart

On Broadway, it's a big brown book full of little black dots. Nashville? Numbers, each representing a chord built on a scale degree in the perfect key for the singer's voice. For guitarists, there's tablature. Violinists, a melodic masterpiece of *mellifluous obbligato*. And for the worship team, usually just chords and lyrics, which necessitates a very good ear!

> *Let us define a chart as "a document consisting of a series of music symbols, giving detailed information that allows for the correct interpretation of a piece of music."*

What's a Chart?

The definition of *chart* is broad and encompasses many communication forms. There are *lead sheets* (lyrics/melody line/chords), *chord charts* (chords with rhythmic notations), *full music scores* (usually piano parts or full orchestration), and the ever-popular *chord/lyric sheet* (chords/lyrics/miscellaneous info).

For our purposes, let's define a chart as *"a document consisting of a series of musical symbols, giving detailed information that allows for the correct interpretation of a piece of music."* Any of the aforementioned chart types can meet this criteria. But only one of these, the chord/lyric sheet, seems to easily facilitate worship team participation without having to actually read music notation.

The Chord/Lyric Sheet

OK, if we're being honest, the chord/lyric sheet is seriously lacking in the way of musical detail; specifically, the melodic line of the song it presents. Since the chord/lyric sheet includes no actual music notation, let's agree that in order to use it we must be willing and able to learn the melody of the song by ear, either by listening to others sing it live, or by practicing with a recording. That being said and agreed upon, the chord/lyric sheet seems to be the favorite mode of communication in many of today's worship contexts. It is fast and easy to create, and doesn't require years of formal music training to read.

10 Essential Parts of the Chart

From the perspective of the chord/lyric sheet, let's take some time to examine the essential elements of *chart anatomy*. Properly applied, these will enable the worship team to learn the song, play it together, then hopefully forget about the chart and get down to the real business of glorifying God. This is the art of the chart.

1. Legal Stuff

Certain elements of a chart are required by law. When creating a chord/lyric sheet, or any other type of chart for that matter, be sure to include the song title, name of the author, *copyright* information including the word "copyright" or the symbol ©, followed by the year of the copyright and the name of the publisher. You'll also need to include the letters *CCLI* (Church Copyright Licensing International), followed by the license number of the church or organization where you'll be using the chart.

2. Road Map

The road map of a song can be communicated with a series of capital letters, which are the first letter of each section heading: I = Intro, V = Verse, C = Chorus, and so on. In what order do we play the chart sections if the road map is as follows: I – V1 – C – V2 – C – O? This would be played: Intro, Verse 1, Chorus, Verse 2, Chorus, Outro.

3. Tempo Marking

The *tempo marking* is usually a single word, such as "fast," "medium," or "slow." (In classical music language, *allegro*, *moderato*, or *adagio*.) It may also be communicated numerically, as in "*quarter note* = 112."

This means to play the song at a tempo of 112 beats per minute, with each quarter note receiving one beat. The tempo can be practiced and rehearsed consistently by listening to the precise click of a *metronome* or *drum loop* while playing the song again and again.

4. Key Signature

When using a chord/lyric chart, the key may be represented simply as: key of C, key of E, and so on.

5. Time Signature

There are two parts to the *time signature*. These include the top and bottom numbers. For example, in 4/4 time, the top 4 tells us that there are four beats in each measure. The bottom 4 indicates that a quarter note receives one beat. Some other time signatures we might commonly encounter in worship songs are 3/4, 2/4, and 6/8.

6. Lyrics

The lyrics of a song are embodied, line by line, in a chord/lyric sheet.

7. Chords

The chords of a song are also included in a chord/lyric sheet. These are aligned with the lyrics, syllable by syllable, to facilitate the correct timing of chordal changes.

8. Section Headings

Section headings coordinate with the road map (see number 2 above, "Road Map") to help the worship musician always be in the right place at the right time, musically speaking.

9. Repeat Signs

Repeat signs [|:   :|] are a handy little device for cutting down on printer's ink. By using repeat signs, we read a particular section more than once during the playing of a song without having to print it again.

10. Additional Directions

Usually bracketed [   ], additional directions such as [repeat chorus] or [to outro] are included in the chord/lyric sheet format to help the worship team move together smoothly from one section to another, or to interpret the music correctly.

Sample Chord/Lyric Sheet

Charts have always been the great unifier of musicians. I'm sure the earliest charts *must* have been scratched on cave walls. Since then, of course, technology has advanced just a little. Figure 6-1 below is a sample worship chord/lyric sheet, embodying the elements 1 through 10 we've just discussed. Understanding the art of the chart is primo for facilitating the effective flow of worship. As you include these chart essentials in your team communications, I pray that you'll be freer than ever from worship distractions and able to keep your eyes unflinchingly fixed on *The Prize*! If you'd like to learn the melody of this song, "Lord, You Care for Me," and perhaps sing it yourself, it can be heard on YouTube at: www.YouTube .com/user/SandyHoffmanMusic.

FIGURE 6-1

LORD, YOU CARE FOR ME - Key of G
Sandy Hoffman

I – V1 – V2 – B – Inst. – B – V1 w/Tag – O
6/8 Time, Moderately Slow

INTRO:
Gno3 D	Cadd9			Gno3 D	Am	Cadd9
///	///	///	///	///	///	///	///

Gno3 D	Em	Cadd9	Gno3/D	D	Gno3 Gno3
///	///	///	///	///	///	///	///

VERSE 1:

Gno3   D   Cadd9   Gno3 D   Am   Cadd9
Lord, You care for me,   / / /   ev'ry   prayer I breathe, You hear

Gno3 D   Em Em/D Cadd9 Gno3/D   D   Gno3
Ev'ry crying need You   meet 'cause, / Lord, You care for me

VERSE 2:

Gno3   D   Cadd9   Gno3   D Am   Cadd9
Lord, You know my heart,   / / /   formed me in my mother's womb

Gno3   D Em Em/D Cadd9 Gno3/D   D   Gno3
How could I be hid from   You 'cause, / Lord, You know my heart

BRIDGE:

[N.C.] D D D2 D Am7   Gno3/B
So I will cast / all my cares on You   /

     Cadd9   D   D2 D   D D2 D
You want me to, You said so, and I   will offer   / / /

Am7   Gno3/B Cadd9 Am7 C/D
All my heart,   /   ev'ry   part to You / / /

continued

continued from previous page

INST:

Gno3 D	Cadd9			Gno3 D	Am	C	
///	///	///	///	///	///	///	///

Gno3 D	Em	Cadd9		Gno3/D	D	Gno3	
///	///	///	///	///		///	///

BRIDGE:

[N.C.] D   D D2 D Am7   Gno3/B
So I will cast / all my cares on You /

    Cadd9   D   D2 D   D D2 D
You want me to, You said so, and I will offer   / / /

Am7   Gno3/B Cadd9 Am7   C/D
All my heart,   /   ev'ry   part to You ///

VERSE 1 W/TAG:

Gno3   D   Cadd9   Gno3 D   Am   Cadd9
Lord, You care for me,   ///   ev'ry   prayer I breathe, You hear

Gno3 D   Em Em/D Cadd9
Ev'ry crying need You   meet 'cause,

Gno3/D   D   Em Em/D Cadd9
Lord, You care for me   /   ///

Gno3/D   D
/ Lord, You care for...

OUTRO:

[|:   Gno3   D   Cadd9   Gno3 D   Am   C
      ///   ///   ///   ///   ///   ///   ///   ///
   ...me

      Gno3   D   Em   Cadd9   Gno3/D D :|]
      ///   ///   ///   ///   ///   ///

      Cadd9 Gno3/B Am7 Gno3
       /   /   /   /
      ritard...   [Hold]

One, Two, Three, Four
(A Simple Sample Song Arrangement)

Playing Favorites

Why is your favorite band your favorite? Do they slam you head-on with a wall of sound like a runaway freight train? Could it be that you enjoy their musical style? Or do you, perhaps, prefer the more gentle approach of the humble honeybee, buzzing contentedly as it flits from flower to flower on a crisp and sunny spring morning, lightly brushing each shimmering petal as the unfolding flora of the fresh new season waltz into full bloo—oh, for Pete's sake! Enough of the schmaltzy nature poetry already! Could it be that your fave band is your fave simply because they know how to treat a song right? (And should I be writing for Disney?)

So what does it mean to treat a song right? What does a simple sample song arrangement look like? Appropriate tempo? Affirmative. Comfortable key? Correct again. How about using the instrumentation that best supports the style and feel of the piece? Yes to style and yes to feel! Does this mean that in order to present worship tunes for their greatest impact, not everyone in the band (or team, in the vernacular) needs to play or sing on every song? Yes, indeed. What we've done here then, is come back around to a "less is more" approach to song arrangement. (Please note that this often requires some serious "dying to self.")

"But," you retort, "isn't it much easier just to cheat by chaotically creating that wall of sound? You know, allow everyone on the team to play and sing all the time?" Sure, it's easier, but just imagine the blessing the worshippers will receive through the tasteful execution of an inspired song arrangement. You know, it's often hard to see the garden when it's surrounded by weeds! How about we remedy that impairment by pulling out the song arranger's hoe and weeding the musical garden 'til all that's left is what really needs to grow there? "And who," you ask, "makes those decisions?" The courageous leader/song arranger, willing to be brutally honest. That's who.

For maximum impact, each song in a worship set list must effectively communicate the mood and the message of the moment to the listener/worshipper. It is the purview of the song arranger to present the heart of the Holy Spirit while preserving the intention of the composer through the skilled and polished performance of the worship composition (whether sequentially predetermined or spontaneously improvised).

> *Each song in a worship set list must effectively communicate the mood and the message of the moment.*

A wise gardener tolerates no weeds! Similarly, a skilled song arranger eliminates extraneous parts and features only the voices and instruments needed to support the musical moment.

Simple Sample Song Arrangement

A great song arrangement, well executed, can turn the sound of a ragtag garage band into a polished presentation! Applying a simple sample song arrangement can make a world of difference in how effectively your worship team connects with the people. We must strive for collective high skill levels, not to be noticed or more appreciated, but to prevent a lack of polish from distracting those we so passionately desire to lead.

Beginning with some sonic information designed to capture the interest of the listener, a praise and worship song will build to subclimax after subclimax. It will then reach the ultimate peak, and finish with an epilogue or outro that allows a bit of time at the end for the worshiper to reflect on the ministry of the Spirit and the gravity of the experience.

One

Now let's begin creating our simple sample song arrangement. To follow along as Sandy explains, please visit: www.YouTube.com/user/SandyHoffmanMusic. Fast or slow, it really doesn't matter. We'll start our hypothetical song with just a keyboard pad. (We don't need to play a honkin' 10-finger chord that sounds like the London Philharmonic.) Just play a simple, two-note string pad. Play both notes using only your right hand (we'll add the left hand a little later), and don't play the two notes close together, like a first and third interval, or a third and fifth. In fact, don't harmonize at all—it's too complex for the moment. Instead, stretch those right-hand fingers from the lower note (thumb) to the higher note (pinky), and play the notes E and E one octave apart. Make sure they're both well above middle C. Mix with prayer and fade in gradually. (Can't you just feel the anticipation building already?)

Two

What's next? Do you think an acoustic guitar might fit into this picture? A simple sample song arrangement in the key of E could easily include a fingerpicked acoustic guitar playing this beautifully ascending/descending chord progression. Each chord in the progression would be played for two beats. Remember, the keyboard is just holding octave Es in the higher register:

$$E - A2 - E - C\sharp m7 - A2/F\sharp - B4 - E - A2.$$

After our keyboard Es have had ample time to slowly fade in and establish themselves, begin to add the acoustic guitar. Cool thing: every one of the chords in this progression includes the note E. Since E is a *common tone* to them all, the keyboard octave Es we're holding will never clash with the chord progression. This creates a wonderfully unifying musical effect. I can't wait for you to try this out for yourself!

Three

The foundation of our hypothetical tune has been laid. Now let's add depth, breadth, and texture! Starting in the lower register, we'll bring in the kick drum on the first and third beat of each *bar*. Next, mirror the kick drum with the bass guitar playing the *root note* of each chord in the progression. Allow two beats for each chord. Remember that the kick drum and bass are *beat buddies*. When it comes to contemporary arrangements, they generally execute the same basic rhythm with only slight variations.

Bass players, did you know that in a chord with something over something, like A2/F$\sharp$ (A2 over F$\sharp$), your bass note is always the note to the right of the slash? In this case, for example, play the alternate bass note, F$\sharp$, while the chorded instruments are playing the A2 chord.

Now let's expand it a bit further by doubling the notes of the bass guitar, playing the same notes on the keyboard. (I told you we'd add the left hand later!) Careful, keyboard, not to play the left hand too loudly. Remember, less is more, and you're doubling the bass notes for breadth and texture, not volume. Playing this progression together, you'll recognize the beginnings of our simple sample song arrangement. Repeat again and again, and worship freely.

Four

Song sections such as verses, choruses, bridges, channels, intros, and outros provide perfect opportunities for creating variations in worship instrumentation and dynamics. Let's have a look at some of these. As the song begins, we'll continue to repeat the chord progression we've already established in our intro with the keyboard, acoustic guitar, then bass guitar and drums.

Starting with verse 1, we'll add in the lead vocal. We'll keep the instrumentation sparse, and as we move from the verse into the *channel* (the section that transitions the verse into the chorus), we'll thin out our instrumentation a bit more. Just when it feels as if we might add, we'll subtract. With the lead vocals continuing, let's use only the keys, acoustic guitar, and a hi-hat on the drums to play the channel. We'll play a different chord progression consisting of: B4 – A2 – B4 – D2.

Each of these chords will be played for four beats instead of the two beats per chord we played in the verse. The channel will build in dynamics until it dramatically morphs into the chorus. Boom! Back in comes the bass guitar, along with the full drum set this time. The electric guitar, slightly overdriven, also joins in with arpeggios (broken chords) as the acoustic guitar begins to strum a steady rhythm:

E – B4 – A2 – A2 – E – B4 – A2 – A2 – D2 – D2 – A2 – A2 – E – B4 – A2 – A2.

Each of the chords in the chorus will receive two beats, which means that when a chord is repeated in the line (like A2 – A2), it is played for a total of four beats. What about the background vocals (BGVs)? Time to go for it! The chorus, being the apex of a good song, is usually the moment when everyone comes in to make their greatest musical impact. And since the chorus almost always plays host to the *hook* (the most memorable words or line in the song), it is very likely the part that people will be singing on the drive home!

We're ready now for verse 2! This is where we lower the dynamics and thin out the instrumentation again. At this point, our hypothetical worship song is beginning to feel like real music. Let the bottom drop out even further as the verse moves into the channel again. This time, as the channel flows into the chorus, the band dynamics can rise to a great climax! Use more movement on the drums, and add percussion instruments like shaker, tambourine, congas, etc. Play a fuller, lower-octave bass guitar, use power chords on the electric guitar, and sing thick, rich vocal harmonies. Fills, licks, and tricks can also be added on *obbligato* (single note) instruments to make the arrangement even more interesting. Now pull out all the stops and play the chorus yet again, this time a little bigger, louder, and even more emotive!

Finishing Well

It's finally time for the tag. Since all or part of the last line of the chorus is usually the hook or song title, why not repeat it a few times at the end of the song to drive home the meaning of the message? This hooky repeat is known as a *tag*, and is a great way to finish big. Try a *ritard* the last time through, gradually slowing the tempo until you land on a huge climactic chord for the perfect grand finale. Hang there a while. Let the big final chord breathe and sustain, allowing people time to think about what they've just sung and Who they've been singing to.

Using many of the methods heard in hit songs for decades, we've created the simple sample song arrangement found in Figure 6-2. Since God is the Redeemer, why not trust Him to redeem these tried and true methods to bring glory to Himself through our worship ministries? Remember to keep it simple, but never be afraid to try out new ideas in worship songs. Arrange to finish well!

FIGURE 6-2

SIMPLE SAMPLE SONG ARRANGEMENT - Key of E

I – V1 – V2 – B – Inst. – B – V1 – Tag – O
4/4 Time, Moderately Slow

INTRO:
[Keyboard in octave notes]

E		E		E		E	
//	//	//	//	//	//	//	//

[Gradually building]

[Acoustic guitar in—keys continue Es]

E	A2	E	C#m7	A2/F#	B4	E	A2
//	//	//	//	//	//	//	//

[Bass guitar and kick drum in]

E	A2	E	C#m7	A2/F#	B4	E	A2
//	//	//	//	//	//	//	//

continued

continued from previous page

[Keyboard left hand in on bass notes]

E	A2	E	C#m7		A2/F#	B4	E	A2
//	//	//	//		//	//	//	//

VERSE 1:

[Lead vocal in]

E	A2	E	C#m7		A2/F#	B4	E	A2
//	//	//	//		//	//	//	//

CHANNEL:

[Lead vocals, keys, acoustic guitar, and hi-hat only]

B4		A2			B4		D2	
//	//	//	//		//	//	//	//

[Gradually building]

VERSE 2:

[Less instruments than in chorus]

E	A2	E	C#m7		A2/F#	B4	E	A2
//	//	//	//		//	//	//	//

CHANNEL:

[Lead vocals, keys, acoustic guitar, and hi-hat only]

B4		A2			B4		D2	
//	//	//	//		//	//	//	//

[Gradually building]

CHORUS 2:

[Instruments like in first chorus—add percussion and lower-octave bass]

E	B4	A2	A2		E	B4	A2	A2
//	//	//	//		//	//	//	//
D2	D2	A2	A2		E	B4	A2	A2

//	//	//	//		//	//	//	//
E	B4	A2	A2		E	B4	A2	A2
//	//	//	//		//	//	//	//
D2	D2	A2	A2		E	B4	A2	A2
//	//	//	//		//	//	//	//

CHORUS 3:

[Even bigger!]

E	B4	A2	A2		E	B4	A2	A2
//	//	//	//		//	//	//	//
D2	D2	A2	A2		E	B4	A2	A2
//	//	//	//		//	//	//	//
E	B4	A2	A2		E	B4	A2	A2
//	//	//	//		//	//	//	//
D2	D2	A2	A2		E	B4	A2	A2
//	//	//	//		//	//	//	//

TAG:

[All instruments and vocals still in]

D2	D2	A2	A2		E	B4	A2	A2
//	//	//	//		//	//	//	//
D2	D2	A2	A2		E	B4	A2	A2
//	//	//	//		//	//	//	//

Part III

CREATING THE CORPORATE CRY

7

Find the Flow
(Enjoying the Experience of Corporate Free Worship)

Schmaltzification, Anyone?

The moment has arrived. The song is ending and the worshipers have been deeply touched. They are now collectively motivated to lift up *encomiums* (high praises) to the Lord. A sweet Spirit is upon the people, and the presence of God is so palpable you could cut it with a knife. You're the lead worshiper. All their eyes are on Jesus, but their expectations lie with you, waiting for that next corporate move in His direction. Now what do you do? At any moment the song will be over. Unless you do something, a dead silence will fall upon the room, a pregnant pause of righteous anticipation. It's your move . . .

> *To schmaltzificate is to fill the void between worship songs, using interesting, Spirit-inspired verbiage and/or instrumental movement.*

Schmaltz•i•fi•ca•tion?

Yes, friends, it's time for schmaltzification! "What in the world is that?!" you may exclaim. *Schmaltzification* is a word coined in the 1990s to help define what happens vocally and/or instrumentally between the programmed songs of a worship set list. To *schmaltzificate* is to fill the void between worship songs, using interesting, Spirit-inspired verbiage and/or instrumental movement. Schmaltzification comes in flavors ranging from the vocally prophetic to the lofty, Spirit-inspired instrumental solo, each sung or played over a repeatable free worship chord progression or *vamp*.

Free Worship Chord Progressions

Free worship chord progressions have a special function in the worship setting. A worship song makes a broad, general statement of praise or adoration to God. But often we feel the need to be more specific than that, more personal than the expressions of a worship composer's lyrics. This is where free worship chord progressions come in handy.

By ending a worship song with a much-repeated chord progression (vamp), we allow the worshipers time to make personal expressions of praise or thanksgiving to God. We flow smoothly from the end of a worship song into the free worship chord progression, and repeat the progression over and over, allowing the worshipers time to personally communicate with God. Because the song and the progression are in the same key and tempo, often the free worship chord progression will lead us right back into the song itself for a more predictable finish.

Free Worship Vocals

Free worship vocals are most often expressed as scripture or prophecy sung over the people, or words of praise and adoration improvised and sung to the Lord. Prayers may also be sung in free form to God. These must be spiritually relevant, and when sung as solos, not be in the framework of our own agendas. They are not *preachy*, but encouraging, bringing blessing to the body of Christ.

Free worship vocals should be musically and stylistically relevant, and in the case of solos, interesting to hear. If the preceding worship song is soft and melodic, our free worship vocals should mimic that. In contrast, rockin', exuberant praise songs bring forth rockin', exuberant free worship. Just follow the lead of the Spirit, and reflect the style of the song. The rest will easily fall into place.

Remember to allow your free worship always to be a catalyst, facilitating the worship of others. Philippians 2:3, 4 (NKJV) tells us to *"Let nothing be done through selfish ambition or conceit, but in lowliness of mind let each esteem others better than himself. Let each of you look out not only for his own interests* (or solos), *but also for the interests of others."* Finally, you may want to use a simple, repeatable melody to start the flow of your free worship. After that, be as musically creative and spiritually expressive as your confidence level allows.

Free Worship Instrumentals

Free worship instrumentals are played as though you're singing. Phrases should rise and fall, allowing time for instrumental breaths in between. This gives a natural human feel to what could become an unending barrage of supersonic arpeggios, runs, and riffs. Let it breathe, and enjoy the dynamic rise and fall of free worship.

Also bear in mind, as always, that less is more. Let's keep our worship instrumentals simple and uncluttered. Overplaying, filling every hole with our sound, can cause us to become a serious distraction to other worshipers. Instead, our prophetic instrumental solos should release the worshipers to express themselves to the Lord (see I Chronicles 25:1-7). Taking others to new heights in their personal and corporate interaction with God is the ultimate human goal of every worship team, every worship time.

Just like free worship vocals, worship instrumentals should be musically relevant, and mirror the style and mood of the preceding worship song. Remember that as the free worship winds down, you may find yourself right back in the song you just came from. It's important to maintain the feel of that song until the team is ready to move on to the next song.

And be dynamic: quiet during quiet, loud during loud. Blasting off into a Hendrixesque guitar solo in the middle of a quiet worship song is probably only going to cause someone to have a worship coronary! Be sensitive to those you're leading into God's presence, or you may find yourself performing a worship defibrillation! Always stay aware of the emotional medium that *is* music.

And then there is skill. Psalm 33:3 (NKJV) instructs us to *"Sing to Him a new song; play skillfully with a shout of joy."* In order to worship freely without distraction, we must really know our instruments. Daily exercise with scales, modes, styles, licks, and tricks is vital to the worship musician. There's a great old saying that goes: "The harder I work, the luckier

I get." As believers, we don't depend on luck. But as Christian musicians, the more time we invest in raising our skill level, the more likely we are to birth fresh ideas, and experience confident execution and creative inspiration during free worship.

As with any other area of our Christian walk, in free worship, God is able to do exceedingly abundantly above all we could ask or think. His unlimited creativity, and desire to draw us closer to Himself, avails His Spirit to us in worship. He motivates, inspires, instructs, and renews. Schmaltzification? I'm convinced that God will meet us there too. How about you?

The Search for Seamless Worship

You've spent hours planning and praying. Your multimedia presentation is second to none. The sound mix is sweet. The worship song list is perfect, and you're ready to go. But after all that preparation, the worship time ends up feeling like stop-and-go traffic with you caught in the gridlock! You know the kind of day I'm talking about. Spiritual warfare, or logistical nightmare? It's often hard to tell, but there is something we can do to help us consistently turn that simple list of worship tunes into a smooth, seamless worship time: find the flow.

Seamless Worship

Let's begin with some definitions. *Seamless worship* is worship that flows from one song to the next, with no stopping in between. We achieve a seamless flow of worship by linking worship songs together with intervals of personal or corporate expression. One way to facilitate this link is through the use of free worship chord progressions.

A *chord progression* is a series of chords played in a predetermined sequence. In Table 7-1, the progression is G, C, D, C. We play it over and over again, assigning two beats to each chord in the progression:

Table 7-1

Chord:	G	C	D	C	G	C	D	C
Beat number:	1, 2	3, 4	1, 2	3, 4	1, 2	3, 4	1, 2	3, 4

A free worship chord progression is a repeatable sequence of chords that is tagged onto the end of a praise or worship song. This tag allows us time for personal expressions of praise and adoration before moving along to the next song. As we become skillful in the flow of seamless worship, our worship times no longer resemble stop-and-go traffic. Instead, they are like wide, smooth highways, effortlessly transporting us into the presence of the Lord!

The Number System

In addition to calling chords by their letter names, G, C, D, and so on, chords can be identified by numbers. Here in Table 7-2, the major chords are uppercase (I), and the minor chords are lowercase (ii).

Table 7-2

Chord:	G	Am	Bm	C	D	Em	F#o	G
Chord number:	I	ii	iii	IV	V	vi	vii	I

In the key of G, the G chord is chord number I. Starting with G and counting up the scale to C makes C the number IV chord and D the number V chord. Now, in Table 7-3, instead of calling it G, C, D, C, we can identify it as the I – IV – V – IV or 1 – 4 – 5 – 4 chord progression:

Table 7-3

Chord:	G	C	D	C	G	C	D	C
Chord number:	I	IV	V	IV	I	IV	V	IV
Beat number:	1, 2	3, 4	1, 2	3, 4	1, 2	3, 4	1, 2	3, 4

It is easy to appreciate the benefit of communicating with the number system. In Table 7-4, we refer to numbers instead of letters to identify the chords in a progression. In this way we are free to use any progression in any key at any time without having to rewrite the music.

Table 7-4

Number:	I	IV	V	IV	I	IV	V	IV
Chord:	C	F	G	F	C	F	G	F
	G	C	D	C	G	C	D	C
	D	G	A	G	D	G	A	G
	A	D	E	D	A	D	E	D
	E	A	B	A	E	A	B	A
	F	B♭	C	B♭	F	B♭	C	B♭

The idea is to become as musically free in our worship flow as possible. We strive for seamless worship, and as we reach it, we're able to forget all our technical mumbo-jumbo, and focus our hearts and minds where they really belong—on Jesus!

Chorded Scales in Common Worship Keys

Now that we understand the concept of assigning numbers to chords, we can begin to visualize and play *chorded scales*. Here in Table 7-5 are six chorded major scales in common worship keys. We should familiarize ourselves with these in order to use them freely in worship. (There will be a test.)

Table 7-5

KEY:	I	ii	iii	IV	V	vi	vii°	(I)
C	C	Dm	Em	F	G	Am	B°	(C)
G	G	Am	Bm	C	D	Em	F♯°	(G)
D	D	Em	F♯m	G	A	Bm	C♯°	(D)
A	A	Bm	C♯m	D	E	F♯m	G♯°	(A)
E	E	F♯m	G♯m	A	B	C♯m	D♯°	(E)
F	F	Gm	Am	B♭	C	Dm	E°	(F)

Chorded Minor Scales Too

We should have a look at chorded scales in the most common minor worship keys. These will also come in handy during free worship. Notice in Table 7-6 their relativity to the major keys of C, G, D, and F.

Table 7-6

KEY	i	ii	III	iv	V	VI	VII	(i)
Am	Am	Bm	C	Dm	E	F	G	(Am)
Em	Em	F#m	G	Am	B	C	D	(Em)
Bm	Bm	C#m	D	Em	F#	G	A	(Bm)
Dm	Dm	Em	F	Gm	A	B♭	C	(Dm)

Using Free Worship Chord Progressions

Now that we've laid the proper foundation, let's apply this number system to communicating free worship chord progressions. These can be used to tie our worship tunes together into a seamless flow. Probably the most common progression used in free worship is I – IV/I – I – IV/I (that's one, four over one, one, four over one). In the key of G the chords are G – C/G – G – C/G.

Always remember, when we say something "over" something, like C/G, the first letter is the name of the chord itself—in this case, C. The second letter, G, is the name of the alternate bass or *root note*. The slash between the letters indicates that we're using a bass note other than the normal root of the chord. This is called an *inversion*. Using the number system, can you figure out the I – IV/I – I – IV/I progression in the key of D? (Here's a HUGE HINT: D – G/D – D – G/D.)

Now let's say we've just finished worshiping with a song like "Come, Now Is the Time to Worship." The next song in our list is "Holy." These songs share the same key, and have similar *tempi*. On the last word of the first song, we begin to play four beats of D, four beats of G/D, four beats of D, four beats of G/D, as shown in Table 7-7:

Table 7-7

I	IV/I	I	IV/I
D	G/D	D	G/D
/ / / /	/ / / /	/ / / /	/ / / /
Come...		Come...	

As we repeat this free worship chord progression, we're allowing time for personal praises to rise. Solo instruments like the piano, electric guitar, winds, or strings may want to join with the vocalists in these moments of heartfelt expression. Then, when we sense from the Holy Spirit that it's time to move on, we can flow right into the next song, "Holy holy/ God almighty/ who was and is to come . . ." Without a hiccup, we've transitioned seamlessly from one song to the next.

This same I – IV/I – I – IV/I progression may also be used to worship in other keys like A and E. Remember, we can play any progression in any key at any time. What a fantastic tool for worship leaders and musicians!

Going Free Worship Super Nova

Now you've got the hang of it. It's time to create your own free worship chord progressions. (I told you there would be a test.) Here in Tables 7-8 through 7-11 are five examples to help get you started.

Practice schmaltzification using these progressions during and between worship songs in the designated keys first, then in any other key and tempo you may choose.

Table 7-8

1.	I (G)	ii (Am)	IV (C)	V (D)
	/ / / /	/ / / /	/ / / /	/ / / /
2.	ii (Am)	IV (C)	I (G)	I (G)
	/ / / /	/ / / /	/ / / /	/ / / /

Try the next one in the key of D.

Table 7-9

3.	I (D)	I^4	I	I^2
	/ / / /	/ / / /	/ / / /	/ / / /

In Table 7-10, try the key of E using Aadd9 and B4/A.

Table 7-10

4.	IVadd9	V^4/IV	IVadd9	V^4/IV
	/ / / /	/ / / /	/ / / /	/ / / /

Now let's play Table 7-11 in a minor key: Am, F, C, G.

Table 7-11

5.	i	VI	III	VII
	/ / / /	/ / / /	/ / / /	/ / / /

While referring to the "Chorded Scales in Common Worship Keys" chart mentioned earlier in Table 7-5, why not spend some time assigning different keys and tempi to each of the preceding examples? Next, try using them to flow between your favorite worship songs. As soon as you're comfortable with that, begin to create your own progressions. The possibilities are limitless, and it won't be long until you and your team have found the flow that ties your worship list together into a powerful, nonstop glory to God!

Maintaining Musical *Mellifluity*

I guess the whole idea is to get the worship team off the page and into the praise. We do whatever it takes to free ourselves from our insecurities and dependence on the chord chart. After all, musical *mellifluity* is about a smooth, rich flow, unencumbered by distraction or distress.

No fear. Soon you'll be freed from the chart to play from the heart.

Does this sound too good to be true? Free to simply worship without fear of flubs or failure? When generously applied, the following essential worship drills will empower your team to move seamlessly from song to free worship time then back to song again. No fear. You'll be freed from the chart to play from the heart.

Common Chorded Scales

It seems that many of today's popular praise and worship tunes are written in one of the six most common worship keys: C, D, E, F, G, or A.

If the song is not in a major key, it is most likely written in one of the minor keys relative to those six common major keys: Am, Bm, Cm, Dm, Em, or F#m.

Most of these are quite common in today's worship setting, and are easily accessible on the guitar—so often the driving instrumental force of the contemporary worship band.

To prepare our team for the drill, let's begin by warming up on chorded scales in common worship keys. We'll start by building a triad on each note of the C major scale: C, D, E, F, G, A, B, C.

By doing so, we end up with the following sequence of chords: C, Dm, Em, F, G, Am, Bdim, C. (See Table 7-5.)

The C major scale has now become the C major chorded scale. Please note that the sequence of chords in a *chorded major scale* is always major, minor, minor, major, major, minor, diminished.

Set your *metronome* to 112 beats per minute and have your entire team play up and back down the C major chorded scale again and again. Allow each chord only two beats before moving to the next. This simple exercise should be repeated in the six most common major worship keys. Once the team has mastered the chorded major scales, repeat the exercise in the four most common minor keys: Am, Dm, Em, and Bm. (See Table 7-6.)

The chordal sequence for minor keys is minor, minor, major, minor, major, major, major. In the key of A minor, for example, the *chorded minor scale* is played: Am, Bm, C, Dm, E, F, G, Am.

Worship Chord Progressions

Now that we've warmed up on some chorded scales in common worship keys, we're ready to move to the more practical common worship chord progressions. Worship chord progressions are used to help facilitate free worship, and to make smooth transitions from one worship song to the next. A worship chord progression can be created by extracting the central, repeatable chord progression from any worship song.

Try this. In the song "Your Grace Is Enough" by Matt Maher, the primary chord progression found in the chorus is: G – D – Em – Cadd9 – G – D – Cadd9 – Cadd9.

Each chord is played for four beats at 118 beats per minute. Try playing this progression over and over with your team. As you play the final Cadd9, prepare to flow straight into the next song, "Forever" by Chris Tomlin, in the key of A. On the leader's signal, go! Smooth? With a little repetitive practice, your transition will become seamless. The distraction of stopping between songs will vanish, and your team and congregation will have time between songs to do three important things:

1. Contemplate the lyrics from "Your Grace Is Enough."
2. Engage in the free expression of praise and worship to God.
3. Prepare for the walloping exuberance of the next song, "Forever."

Major Flow

Any chord progression may be played in any key. Through simple *transposition*, we can end a song, for instance, in the key of D, then with a repeatable worship chord progression, move right up to the key of E and into the next song. Using a couple of popular Paul Baloche tunes, let's try this essential worship drill together. First, end the song "I Will Boast" (key of D) with a simple, repeatable progression: D4 – D – D4 – D.

Each chord is played for two beats. When you're ready, simply pop right up to the key of E and continue playing the same worship chord progression: E4 – E – E4 – E.

Feel free to hang there while individual worship takes place. During this time, team members may be inspired to take turns playing improvised *worship solos* to the Lord. Just let it breathe, and when the transition feels complete, move to the next song, "All The Earth Will Sing Your Praises!" You are already in the correct key.

At this point, the worship team should be getting more comfortable with free worship and worship transitions. They're no longer glued to the page and hanging on for dear life. Instead, the freedom of worship flow without fear is emerging.

Minor Flow

Let's look at another free worship example, this time in a minor key. There's a favorite song about the cross of Christ. Written by Matt Redman and Beth Redman, it's called "For the Cross" (released on *The Heart of Worship* CD). The recorded arrangement is in the key of B minor, and includes a free worship moment that truly moves the soul. We use it often on communion Sundays to express our profound appreciation for the eternal life-giving love of Jesus. The arrangement flows from the chorus, "And I love You for the cross . . .", into a free worship chord progression consisting of Bm, Gadd9, A2/F#, and Gadd9.

After giving ample time to offer thanks to the Lord for His completed work, the song returns to the chorus for an emotionally charged ending. I suggest taking time for the team to worship together with this progression. Set your metronome at 110 beats per minute and linger there, offering your highest praises to the Only One Worthy. Afterward, you might lower and raise this progression to other minor worship keys, repeating them many times until you become fluent in the language of *mellifluous* worship.

Overflow!

To be *mellifluous* (smooth, rich, and flowing) in our worship times requires practice and repetition on the part of the worship team. We must be intentional as we strive for a balance between premeditated creativity and spontaneous free worship expression. That smooth, rich flow of worship that beckons the followers of Jesus to come into the Holy of Holies will certainly happen as we maintain our musical mellifluity.

Jammin' to Gel

Then David and all the house of Israel played music before the Lord on all kinds of instruments made of fir wood, on harps, on stringed instruments, on tambourines, on sistrums and on cymbals.

—II Samuel 6:5 (NKJV)

Garage Band Jam

I can't get this vision out of my head: I'm walking down a long gravel driveway, ending at an old, dilapidated, whitewashed garage. There's a dirt floor. Music of a most extraordinary nature is emanating from every termite hole in the place. Enticed by the sound, I am compelled to investigate. The door swings open, and suddenly I'm face to face with—you guessed it—a bunch of guys (it's probably Saturday night). Each one has an instrument in hand, and every one of their facial expressions is different. Some are focused and serious, some are smiling, others are offering warm greetings, and still others are completely ignoring me. They've convened for a singular purpose: to jam. They are there to allow their musical imaginations to run wild, unfettered by charts or direction or spectators. They are truly a garage band!

> *Jamming brings unity of sound, dynamic sensitivity, freedom from inhibition, interpersonal consideration and awareness, and often stimulates some pretty amazing creativity.*

Webster's calls *jamming* "an impromptu performance by a group of musicians that is characterized by improvisation." In the worship vernacular, I like to think of it as improvisation by inspiration. No matter how we define it, one thing is certain: when our worship team spends some time jammin' together like the band in the whitewashed garage, it really helps us to gel. Jamming brings unity of sound, dynamic sensitivity, freedom from inhibition, interpersonal consideration and awareness, and often stimulates some pretty amazing creativity. Coupled with inspiration from the Holy Spirit, we get to enjoy a win-win-win situation! Spiritually, relationally, and musically, we grow when we're jammin' to gel.

Effective Exercise

Last night we rehearsed. One minute we were singing "Rock of Ages, Jesus Is the Rock" by Rita Baloche, the next we'd morphed into that old familiar garage band again, covering a Beatles tune of course: "Chains, my baby's got me locked up in chains, and they ain't the kind that you can see," from the 1963 album *Please Please Me*. This happens often in our rehearsals, and for a very good reason: we're *gellin'*! What may appear to the uninitiated as dabbling in secular—or at best, time-wasting—reminiscences, can actually become quite an effective exercise, greatly enhancing team cohesion and flow.

First, Honor God

Did you notice in the first half of II Samuel 6:5 that "*. . . David and all the house of Israel played music before the Lord . . .*"? The focus here is: "*before the Lord.*" Their apparent intention was to celebrate the return of the ark of God by jammin' in His presence. In one translation it says they were honoring Him, in others, they were celebrating with songs on their instruments. One even mentions dancing and singing with all their might. In other words, their hearts were in it, and their passion for the presence of God was made manifest through their improvisational music expression. Here is Biblical precedent for communicating the depths of our joy in the Lord through instrumental praise. Israel jammed and gelled!

Now Gel the Jammers

Right about now, you're probably saying to yourself, "This all sounds great, but how do we get from jammin' to gellin' with our team?" Glad you asked. Here are five practical suggestions I trust will help facilitate some God-honoring jammin' right where you live.

1. Never Fear

Never fear to wander off the beaten path. At least during rehearsals, feel free to play whatever songs emerge. Often, between the programmed songs in the set, someone will begin to noodle around on an old familiar tune. When this happens, seize the moment and let the song take you where it will. Make it your own, and take turns being the leader or soloist. Some very usable song arrangements and secular lyric revisions (redemptions) have come out of this type of jammin'. Remember that creativity has a mind of its own. It sometimes strikes when you least expect it. Go with the inspirational flow, and you may be surprised with the long-term usable results.

2. Flow Out

Flow out of a praise and/or worship song into a congruent, repeatable chord progression. Take turns soloing over the progression. Be dynamic in the flow, rising and falling in volume and intensity as inspired by the Holy Spirit. Maintain awareness of the parts others are playing around you, and defer to one another as each enjoys the opportunity to express their instrumental passion through praise to the Lord. When you're finished, you may easily flow back into the praise or worship song where you started.

Jammin' to gel is just plain fun.

3. Singers Can Jam

Singers can jam too! Try singing prophetically over the repeatable chord progression, expressing instantaneously inspired lyrics and melodies to honor and celebrate God. Scriptures supported by an inspired melody may also be sung over a repeatable chord progression. Open up the Psalms, find one that fits contextually, and begin to sing it with all your might. Lift it up just as David and all the house of Israel did before the Lord. Now you're joining in the everlasting song!

4. Remember It's OK

Remember that it's OK to build a song arrangement, even when you're jammin'. It's not necessary for everyone to play at every moment. Defer, defer, defer. Consciously practice leaving holes—silent spaces for no one in particular to fill. Music consists of two basic elements: notes and rests. We can't expect our notes to communicate effectively if we ignore those all-important moments of silence in our songs.

5. Let the Rhythm Section Carry You

Let the rhythm section, primarily bass and drums, carry your jam along. They create the foundation for the other players (actors) to make entrances, say (play) their lines, then exit. Each player should endeavor to leave a gaping hole for the next one to fill.

Jammed and Gelled

Some of my fondest memories as a musician, and especially as a worshiper, are related to jam sessions. You've gotta give it a try. Jammin' to gel is just plain fun. At the same time, it stimulates the individual musician, sets the inhibited free, and it will cause your team to become tighter than they ever were before!

8

Make the Mod (and Let His Praises Rise Together)

Six Degrees of Worship Keys

Ever planned a worship time with six songs all in the same key? After about the fourth tune, even the praise team is yawning. Occasionally this happens, but why? It may be the simple fact that the worship leader doesn't have a grasp of *chordal modulations*. When we stay in the same safe key from song to song, our worship times can become flat and lifeless. Modulating after a tune or two brings lift and life back to worship. As worship leaders, our goal is to facilitate, not manipulate; but we do need to be as clever as possible as we endeavor to keep our worship times interesting and engaging. Modulating upward from time to time is an effective device in our quest to provoke passionate praises.

So we've found ourselves almost always worshiping in the keys of C, D, E, F, G, and A, haven't we? How did that happen? As worship music has become more guitar-based in nature, so have our favorite keys. These six keys seem to lend themselves best to our guitar-driven praise. They fall comfortably under the fingertips, and generally make the most of the sonic qualities of the guitar. Even when we're using a capo to cheat and play in a flat or sharp key, we're still using the same left-hand fingerings found in the six degrees of worship keys. (I assure you, this chapter is not just for guitarists!)

Now that we've identified today's most common worship keys, we're left with two very important questions to answer (maybe three):

1. What is the relationship of one key to another?
2. How do we move seamlessly from key to key?

And a possible third question:

3. What do we do with all those other keys we have left over?

Key Relationships

C, D, E, F, G, and A are the first six notes in the C major scale. The six most common worship keys are rooted in the first six scale degrees of the key of C. Each key is named after a note in the C scale: C, D, E, F, G, and A. In reference to these six common worship keys, let's answer question number one, "How do these keys relate to one another as we ascend the C scale by degrees?"

- Chords in the key of C (which has no sharps or flats) are one whole step lower than the corresponding chords in the key of D.
- Chords in the key of D (which has two sharps: F-sharp and C-sharp) are one whole step lower than the corresponding chords in the key of E.
- Chords in the key of E (which has four sharps: F-sharp, C-sharp, G-sharp, and D-sharp) are one half step lower than the corresponding chords in the key of F.
- Chords in the key of F (which has one flat: B-flat) are one whole step lower than the corresponding chords in the key of G.
- Chords in the key of G (which has one sharp: F-sharp) are one whole step lower than the corresponding chords in the key of A.
- Chords in the key of A (which has three sharps: F-sharp, C-sharp, and G-sharp) are one-and-a-half steps lower than the corresponding chords in the key of C.

Hey! Why are we leaving out the key of B? We're answering question number three a little early here, but because of its plethora of *barre chord*–inducing sharps, the key of B seems only occasionally to show up in contemporary praise. The same goes for other left over/left out keys. The main exception, of course, is when we cheat and use a capo on the guitar. In this way we're actually playing in the flat or sharp keys, but we're fingering the chords as though they were in one of those six most common worship keys.

Chordal Modulations

Now let's answer question number two. How do we move seamlessly from one worship key to the next? Here are five quick tips for moving up the scale, always changing keys in a heavenly direction!

1. Use a pivotal chord.

Using the number system in the key of C, C is I, F is IV, and G is V. To move from the key of C to the key of D (up one whole step), use the IV/V chord (that's "four over five") in the new key (D) as a pivotal chord between the two keys. Now play: C – F – G – G/A – D – G – A.

Remember, something "over" something (like G/A) means that the chord we play is G, but we're using an alternate bass note, A, instead of the regular root note, G. By using the pivotal, or transitional, chord, we've moved seamlessly from the key of C to the key of D. This works in all the other keys as well. Gold mine! (See "The Search for Seamless Worship" in Chapter 7, "Find the Flow," for more information on the number system.)

2. Go straight up a fourth.

Especially on the guitar, fourths are really easy to remember. From the lowest string, E, to the next string, A, is a fourth. Fourths also occur when moving from the A to the D string and from the D to the G string. Let's say you begin a worship time with the song "Forever," by Chris Tomlin in the key of A. When you're ready, you can move right up to the key of D and play a song like "I Will Boast," by Paul Baloche. Fourths always provide us with a smooth transition from one worship song to the next.

3. Let the IV chord in the old key become the I chord in the new key.

Try playing "You Are So Good to Me," by Don Chaffer and Ben and Robin Pasley, in the key of E. End on the IV chord, A, instead of the I chord, E. Now go right into "Mighty to Save," by Reuben Morgan and Ben Fielding, in the key of A, and you'll enjoy a wonderfully smooth transition!

4. Let the V chord in the old key become the I chord in the new key.

Let's try using "Mighty to Save" in the key of A once again. This time, we'll end on the V chord, E, instead of the I chord, A. It's a clever way to set up for the next song, "Our Love Is Loud," by David Crowder, which happens to be in the key of E. No stopping and starting between songs, just seamless praise to our worthy God!

5. Go straight up one half step or one whole step.

Finally, why not jump straight up from the key of G to A or from the key of E to F? This works especially well when changing keys within a song, between verses or choruses.

A solid understanding of key relationships and chordal modulations is a powerful tool for facilitating the flow of worship. As we apply this music theory to our earthly times of praise, we'll begin to see the heavenly fruit that most certainly blossoms in the lives of those we lead into God's holy presence.

Lower Keys for Worship Ease

Maybe it's about mercy. You know, putting an end to all those purple faces and bulging eyeballs. And no, I'm not talking about hyperventilation or taking scuba-diving lessons. It's those stratospheric keys we seem to be singing our worship songs in! Why not bring 'em down so we can take that silly announcement about *post-service collective resuscitation* out of the bulletin every Sunday? Let's lower our worship keys for worship ease.

Purple Faces/Bulging Eyes

Recently we introduced an award-nominated worship song to our list. It was powerfully anointed and extremely well received. The writer has been recognized for years as one of the most prolific and profound writers in the worship world. He's an awesome songwriter! But he, like many others, has displayed one other outstanding trait: an extreme high-end vocal range. We tried the song in *his* key, but even among the best worship team singers, we began to notice that purple face/bulging eyes effect.

What's Your Tessitura?

The average comfortable pitch range, or tessitura, is from middle C on the keyboard up one octave, or eight white keys, to the next highest C. This particular worship song topped out at a whopping high G. That's an interval of three and one-half steps above the average congregational *vocal range*; enough to strain even the warmest voice. Because the writer was also a gifted singer, that tessitura was no big deal for him. But considering that the bulk of our local worship expression occurs during the vocally cold morning hours, there was really only one obvious congregational remedy: lower the key.

Who Needs Modulation?

In common modulations, or key changes, we are usually focused on moving the key up a half step, whole step, or some other interval that raises the song to new heights. Often, worship modulation is used to build excitement and energy from chorus to chorus or song to song. But when we're making our worship range more accessible to the average voice, we really don't need to modulate upward at all. Instead, we pitch the song in a lower key to start with, and probably remain there. If we keep the average vocal range of C to C in mind, we can create a vocal comfort zone for all those who worship. After that, it's "Bye-bye Sunday morning vocal strain."

We're Talking Transposition

What we're really talking about here is transposition. We're lowering the key of the worship song so most people can sing it comfortably. Remember, the easier we make the execution, the more fully the people participate.

As a kid in the Southern Baptist church, I loved to sing the old hymns. But going home after church, I'd often notice that I had a bit of a sore throat. Have you ever paid attention to the tessitura of some of your favorite hymns? Songs like "'Tis So Sweet to Trust in Jesus" (D to D), "There Is Power in the Blood" (F to E-flat), and "Make Me a Blessing" (C to F)? These are real *neck stretchers*. Many of us couldn't possibly reach those high notes if we were standing on a chair! What's needed in many traditional hymns, and not a few of today's praise and worship songs, is transposition in the downward direction.

So Let's Drop It

What are the nuts and bolts of this type of transposition? In essence, we move all the chords in a song's chord progression downward, applying the same intervallic movement to each. Hypothetically, if the song is pitched in the key of A, with a (vocal) tessitura of D to D, we might try lowering it a whole step to the key of G. The pitch range for singers would then become C to C. As we drop each chord one whole step, as shown in Tables 8-1 and 8-2, the entire melody is also transposed to the more singable lower key.

Original key of A:

Table 8-1

A	D2	E	A
/ /	/ /	/ /	/ /

New key of G (one whole step lower):

Table 8-2

G	C2	D	G
/ /	/ /	/ /	/ /

Let's lower another worship chord progression. This time, let's say the song is written in the key of C, but we'd like to sing it one and one-half steps lower, in the key of A. We'll imagine that our highest vocal note is D. By dropping the key of the song one and one-half steps, our highest note becomes a much more comfortable B. We no longer strain to gain and maintain that high pitch. Instead, our thoughts are concentrated on what is really important: honoring God. Let's try the following (merciful) key change, found in Tables 8-3 and 8-4.

Original key of C:

Table 8-3

C	F	Dm7	G
////	////	////	////

New key of A (one and one-half steps lower):

Table 8-4

A   D   Bm7   E

/ / / /   / / / /   / / / /   / / / /

They'll Thank You!

With a little practice, you'll become adept at transposition. It will soon be second nature to recognize the red flags of vocal aeronautics. You'll start to respond to them by bringing the key of a worship song back down to earth. Once on solid ground, the people you're leading will be able to sing without that vocal distraction. With deep appreciation, they'll focus on something greater than the pain of vocal strain, and they'll thank you for it! Always enjoy listening to those incredible studio versions of your favorite worship songs, no matter how stratospheric, but don't hesitate to lower the key for those you are leading. Sometimes it's necessary to create a vocal comfort zone, making it much easier for the people to sing their praises to the Most High.

9

Lead and Be Led
(in Every Area of Life by Personal Leadership and Humility)

Worship Leader/Followers

Lead, follow, or get out of the way! I'm not sure I agree with that "get out of the way" attitude, but at any moment, in every area of our lives, we are leading, following, or both.

As worship leaders, we publicly exercise the principles of corporate leadership. As worship followers, we keep our eyes on Jesus, watching and waiting intently for the Spirit's every move. There's a powerful partnership between the Lord and the leader. We lead as we follow, and we follow as we lead.

A Perfect Example

No doubt you're familiar with the story of King Jehoshaphat in II Chronicles Chapter 20. Here's a man who has yielded his kingly authority to God. He's a leader of the people and a follower of the Lord. Perfect! But just to make things interesting, add three armies to the mix and have them decide to rise up against the king and wipe out the people he leads. Can you guess what the king's immediate response was? He felt the same way any one of us would feel in a similar situation: fearful. In spite of his anxiety, he set himself to seek the Lord. He had the good sense to know it was time to move quickly from leader to follower mode.

As the story unfolds, the Lord gives the prophet Jahaziel a word for the people of Judah. He tells them not to be afraid, and that the battle belongs to the Lord. Then a powerful thing happens. The king bows his head with his face to the ground. Suddenly, he's become a lead worshiper! And all Judah and the inhabitants of Jerusalem bow before the Lord, worshiping the Lord.

Then the Levites stood up to praise the Lord God of Israel with voices loud and high. They became lead worshipers too. Can't you just see them standing and shouting with fists in the air, proclaiming God's might and power on the day before the battle? What a scene!

From start to finish, Jehoshaphat embodied both the authority of a king and the humility of a servant. The result was victory for God's people. Like him, we should be leading with authority and following with humility, instructing and releasing others as we go. We lead as we follow, and we follow as we lead.

Leader/Follower Checklist

We've established the Biblical precedent for the dual role of leader/follower. Now let's talk about some practical habits, some in review, which will keep us ready to function as both.

1. Be Spiritually Prepared and Focused

Over the years, one lesson I've learned that outshines many others is, *what goes in is what comes out.* If I'm not filling my mind with God thoughts and God dreams, then I won't have any God substance to share with anyone else. In Deuteronomy 6:6-9 (NKJV) God relates to us the importance of always contemplating His Word and will: *"And these words which I command you today shall be in your heart; you shall teach them diligently to your children, and shall talk of them when you sit in your house, when you walk by the way, when you lie down, and when you rise up."*

Not too long ago I spent three days fully engaged in the pages of a current best-seller. This was unusual for me, but because of the national hubbub over the book, I felt the need to know its content. I wanted to be relevant. Once I started to read it, I found I couldn't put it down. Every time I got to the end of a chapter I simply had to know what came next. After contemplating this faith-challenging, philosophical goop from Thursday to Saturday, I was expected to be ready to lead worship in three God-honoring services the next morning. It was tough. One minute I'd be totally focused on the Lord and His people, the next my mind was wandering off on some irrelevant tangent from that book. The services proceeded with no apparent glitch, but as I wrestled with my thoughts, it was a powerful reminder that what goes in really is what comes out. As worship leader/followers we must keep His Word in our heads—always!

Psalm 1:1a, 2 (NKJV) says, *"Blessed is the man who walks not in the counsel of the ungodly, nor stands in the path of sinners. But his delight is in the law of the Lord, and in His law he meditates day and night."*

This is where leader/followers have to abide: meditating in His law (Word) day and night.

2. Worship Warm

Though I've covered this subject in depth earlier, I must say again how vital it is that we warm up before we worship! Worshiping warm means spending time with God and maintaining musical discipline. Through daily devotion, instrumental engagement, and vocal vitality, we keep our hearts, hands, and voices always ready to lead (and follow) in worship. We are spiritual athletes: skilled, disciplined, stretched, and focused on one thing—His glory!

3. Live the Life

If you don't know where you're going, any road will get you there. That's why personal and team mission statements are so necessary and why they should be repeated time and time again. In order to live the kind of life that Romans 12:1 says is our *"reasonable act of worship,"* we need a clear, memorable mission statement that defines who we are and what we do. Years ago the Lord made it obvious to me that my life's purpose is: "To go before the throne [of God] and take others with me." Since then, it's been so much easier to evaluate my daily activities and to prioritize them accordingly.

Your Leader/Follower Mission

I'd like to challenge you to consider your spiritual preparedness, daily warm-up habits, and most of all, your godly mission in life. If you haven't done so already, take some time to list the most important Biblical values upon which you base your life. With these in mind, ask yourself, "Who am I?" and "What am I doing?" From the answers to these questions, you should be able to prayerfully create your own mission statement. You may say, "I already have a mission statement for my team." But what about for *yourself*? Shouldn't you have a clear understanding of which road in life you're traveling and what your purpose in worship life is as you travel down that road?

I believe we owe it to ourselves and the Lord to become the very best worship leader/followers we can be. As we establish and maintain our spiritual focus, worship warm-ups, and life mission, we'll be able to do just that.

Arranged to Flow

Effective, Seamless Song Lists

As a worship leader, what is the secret to creating a seamless worship song list? Several important elements must come together to facilitate a worship time that both honors God and motivates the worshiper. A well-thought-out list is like a wide, smooth highway, effortlessly transporting us into the presence of God. A worship song list without flow is like a car with three flat tires. It may get you where you're going, but you probably won't enjoy the ride!

Systematic Song Selection

The Simple Sample Song List

Please circle the worship song that does not belong in the following list:

1. Holy, Holy, Holy (Key of C)

2. Holy (Key of D)
3. Pass It On (Key of Z-flat minor)
4. Open the Eyes of My Heart (Key of E)
5. Holy and Anointed One (Key of G)

If you chose "Pass It On," you are correct. Below are three common criteria that can be used in systematic worship song selection. In our Simple Sample Song List, "Pass It On" summarily fails in all three. Perhaps you used one or more of these criteria to arrive at *your* decision.

Choose by Topic

When preparing a worship song list, we must first prayerfully consider the subject matter. Unless we're shooting for a good old generic worship time (whatever that is), we should begin with a very clear direction in mind. If the worship time precedes a speaker, it's a great idea, at the very least, to meet and pray with them beforehand. This empowers us to put together a relevant list that softens hearts to hear the Word and supports the spoken message. Worship and the Word usually go hand in hand. Often during preparation, the Lord will remind us of Scriptures that support the topic. These can be spoken between songs or during *free worship* times to reinforce the message.

In our Simple Sample Song List, the topic is the Lord's holiness. Consequently, "Pass It On," groundbreaking 1960s classic by Kurt Kaiser that it is, simply won't work in this context. It's a song about God's love and sharing God's love. The whole point of topical flow is to keep the heart and mind of the worshiper focused and moving in a singular direction; in this case, God's holiness.

List by Tempo

Most often, our worship times begin with fast songs and end with slow ones. First praise, then worship, usually with a moderate-tempo pivotal song in the middle. With this in mind, "Pass It On" receives strike two for less-than-perfect tempo placement. It is actually slower than song number four, "Open the Eyes of My Heart." As song number three, "Pass It On" just doesn't make good pacing sense.

Remember however that this song-pacing formula, though common, is not set in cement. Feel free to experiment with lots of tempo variations. You might begin a worship time with slower songs and a time of communion, for example, then move into high praise in celebration of the completed work of Christ. God is the creator. We're designed to co-create with Him. Feel free to exercise imagination by [His] inspiration!

Move Keys Steadily Upward

The third test of a strong worship list is key compatibility. Our list should always be moving us upward in the direction of God's throne (see Hebrews 10:19-23). The first two songs in the sample praise and worship list are in the keys of C and D. Songs number four and five are in the keys of E and G.

If we remove number three, "Pass It On," which for our purposes is in the humorously fictitious key of Z-flat minor, we experience a steady climb from C to D to E to G. These key changes can easily be executed with the use of a pivotal IV/V chord in each new key, or in most cases, by simply going straight up one half-step or one whole step from the old key to the new (see Chapter 8: Make the Mod, "Six Degrees of Worship Keys").

The Elements

Each element of the worship song list should unite with other elements to support the ultimate purpose of our praises: to glorify God and enjoy Him forever! Topic, tempo, and key compatibility must all cooperate to facilitate ease and flow in the worship time. This helps to remove worship road hazards and paves that highway that leads us boldly to the throne of God.

Dos, Don'ts, and Things to Avoid

Now we're ready to put some of our personal and corporate worship habits under the microscope. As Will Rogers once said, "Good judgment comes from experience, and experience comes from bad judgment!" If we look together at some worship dos, don'ts, and things to avoid, it might help us develop a more fruitful worship-planning process and circumvent some of the pitfalls that could come from bad judgment.

Do's

1. Choose and use quality praise and worship songs.

The ground floor of compelling corporate worship is quality worship songs. By choosing and using well-crafted, anointed tunes, we reinforce the worship foundation beneath us.

2. Trust someone to give you an honest song critique.

Are you a songwriter? That's awesome. But just how awesome is up to the listener, not the writer. Please spare your congregation the *worship song guinea pig syndrome*! Good songwriters follow a process of layered critiquing. First, share your new worship tune with a friend or two who will be completely honest with you. If your close friends like it, then maybe you should try it out in a home fellowship setting. Are people asking to hear the song again? Perhaps now it's time to play it for the congregation. Always be honest with yourself!

3. Memorize the words and music.

The best way to stay focused on the Lord in worship is to remove all other distractions, including reading the music during a worship time. Good practice habits enable us to memorize our words and music. This frees us up to think about the Lord, listen to the Spirit, and lead the people. Never hide behind a music stand.

Don'ts

1. Don't manipulate; facilitate.

Leadership is an honor conferred upon the leader by the people. With leadership comes authority, and with authority comes responsibility. As lead worshipers we must provide a safe environment for people to express their deepest, most intimate feelings to God. It's not about having them clap when we say, "Clap," shout when we say, "Shout," or weep when we say, "Weep." It's about giving people permission to sincerely express their hearts to the Lord without fear of manipulation. Always facilitate!

2. Don't use words without meaning.

What's the all-time record for shouting "Hallelujah" during a single worship time? "Praise the Lord!"? "Amen!"? I don't know, but any one of us might qualify for the first-place prize. As lead worshipers, we don't want to become honorary members of the "Department of Redundancy Department." How do we avoid that distinction? Recording and listening back honestly to our worship times is a perfect way to weed out those repetitive words and phrases. Ask the Lord for fresh Scripture and insight for each new worship time. Make this your rule: no worship *filler*!

Avoid

1. Wrong Keys

Be merciful to worshipers with low voices. Take advantage of every opportunity to pitch high songs a bit lower. Remember, they'll thank you for it!

2. Wrong Song Sequence

CAUTION: Moving suddenly from quiet worship into loud, boisterous praise has been known to cause a worship coronary in some lab animals! Be sensitive to the ears and nervous systems of those you are leading.

3. Wrong Chords or Style

For correct chords, do your homework. There are many reference books, DVDs, and websites dedicated to teaching contemporary worship chord voicings. For correct style, listen to existing recordings, then modify the original arrangement to one that is relevant to the people you are leading.

4. Wrong Tempo

Make sure the speed supports the message. We don't gleefully sing about the Crucifixion any more than we play "The Happy Song" by Delirious like a funeral march. Always be appropriate.

What About Rule Number Five?

Psalm 25:9b (NKJV) says, *". . . the humble He teaches His way."* Rule number five? *"Humble yourself in the sight of the Lord* (in humility, be a worship follower) *and He will lift You up."* In His strength, be a worship leader. Remember, we lead as we follow, and we follow as we lead. In the balance of authority and servanthood, we guide others to fall at the feet of Jesus.

Leave 'Em Wantin' More (Creating a Worship Hunger)

Ever experience a worship time that drags on and on? Like Elvis, the Holy Spirit seems to have left the building 10 minutes ago, but the band didn't get the message?

> *In some situations it's abundantly obvious that the team has never really considered the effectiveness of understatement.*

It becomes a marathon, a contest to see how many times we can repeat the same chorus. At this point, the goals of the worship time have been met, and the people are bleary-eyed from reading the lyrics projected on the screen. You're probably standing in the back of the room yourself, scratching your head and wondering why in the world it's not over yet! Your stomach is growling, your mind is wandering, and your feet have begun to throb.

OK, I am exaggerating a bit, but in some situations it's abundantly obvious that the team has never really considered the effectiveness of understatement. Words like louder, longer, bigger, and stronger can take on some pretty undesirable meanings when considered in the context of worship overindulgence. What's needed is a remedy for this sometimes pervasive worship malady. Remembering that too much is always too much, let's agree to define this illness as *run-on worship*. Now the question is, what's the cure?

If we intend to connect with the people and see them return for the next worship time, we've got to leave 'em wantin' more! That doesn't mean we stop the worship time before the Lord is finished with us. If we do that, we'll create a spiritual cliffhanger, a vacuum that may not be filled for days or weeks. In that case the worshipers would indeed be left wanting more, but they may not return to receive all that the Lord has planned for them. I believe there's a better, healthier way to create a hunger for worshiping God in the congregation. We simply need to include some vital ingredients before and during each opportunity we have to lead worship. Staying mindful of these three—inspiration, preparation, and presentation—will help us to plan and lead worship times that will meet the needs of the people and bring them back the next time. When they return, they'll be hungering for more of the corporate presence of the Lord in worship.

Inspiration

Feeling uninspired? Unable to get focused on your next worship time? First, pray. Ask the Lord for His specific heart and anointing of your worship direction. The Scripture says call upon Him in truth and He will draw near to you. He's always there to direct us when we trust Him to do so (see Proverbs 3:5, 6).

Read any good Scripture lately? A daily dose of Bible meditation will make you *"like a tree planted by the river of living waters"* (see Psalm 1:3). When the spiritual nutrients flow downstream from the Lord, your roots will be there, ready to soak up the nourishment and inspiration found in the flow of His freshly revealed Word.

What's going on in your own life—troubles, blessings, both? Allow life's circumstances and challenges to be reflected in the worship you lead. People respond best to those who lead sincerely out of real-life experiences. Many times I've had people come up to me after a worship time and share that the things that were said between the songs ministered to them even more than the songs themselves. Reality speaks volumes. You genuinely connect with people when you're open and vulnerable. The day-to-day issues we face as believers in Christ and the solutions we receive from Him are enough to inspire us with a lifetime of praises to God.

Stay plugged in to the lives of the people you're leading. Up-to-the-minute awareness of the needs of the body for healing, repentance, forgiveness, relational reconciliation (vertical or horizontal), mission, or provision will inspire you to plan and lead an effective worship ministry.

What's the teacher teaching? A wonderful way to find inspiration for worship is to plan in tandem with the teacher/preacher. Meditate on the Scriptures, the ones the teaching is being taken from. You'll be amazed at the powerful partnership that forms when the pastor, worship leader, and Holy Spirit are working together!

Preparation

The first step of preparation is to pray—again! Prayer is the common denominator in leading the type of worship that creates a worship hunger.

Now that you've been inspired, begin to plan a worship set list that supports the heart and topic of your inspiration. Be sure to double-check your list for worship flow. You'll probably want to begin with up-tempo praise, move into a pivotal moderate-tempo song or two in the middle, then end with deeply heartfelt worship songs. Remember to always be moving up the musical scale from song to song—in the direction of heaven.

Now it's communication time. Pull, create, or download the necessary music charts for your team, making sure that you're familiar with all the nuances of each tune before your rehearsal.

Rehearsal? Oh, yes. That vital, sometimes missing, link between the people and a worship time that leaves them wanting more is rehearsal. Please don't wait until Sunday morning for this. Leave some days between rehearsal and ministering in order to have time for that other massively important element of preparation: personal practice. Is it possible to overprepare? I seriously doubt it.

Presentation

To quote the Beatles on *Sgt. Pepper*: "We've been some days in preparation, a splendid time is guaranteed for all." Like the Beatles, we've prepared. Now it's time to present, making use of the "Five Ups" method:

Warm up
Dress up
Pray up
Offer up
Wrap it up!

Warm up. Get those hands and voices ready for worship without injury! Dress up. Looking sharp will enhance the presentation of the worship ministry, helping to remove visual distractions. Don't forget to factor in modesty. Pray up with the team. Ask God for His anointing of hearts, hands, and voices. Next, offer up your very best to God. Be there spiritually, emotionally, and musically. He deserves it!

And now, the big one (drum roll here): wrap it up! No more run-on worship. Being sensitive to the leadership of the Holy Spirit, and to the needs of the people, we will be able to sense when the worship time is over. Ending won't feel awkward, it will just feel right. No confusion, no doubts, no second-guessing. We've done our homework. We're inspired and prepared. And with absolute confidence in our presentation, we leave 'em wantin' more.

What Must I Know?
(Identifying the *True* Worship
Team Essentials)

With easy access to new worship songs, charts, teachings, workshops, instructional materials, software, recording gear, magazines, CDs, DVDs, downloads, websites, and even fine musical instruments, we can easily find ourselves suffering from information/resource overload. Maybe you're like so many others who are wondering, "Just what are the true essentials for worship team leaders and members?" In our culture, which prides itself on thinking in terms of "less is more," perhaps we're all beginning to realize that too much is (still) too much! In the next five paragraphs, we will attempt to cut through a lot of the confusion and establish some absolute essentials for every worshiper.

1. Know the Lord

Matthew 22:37, 38 (NKJV) says, *"You shall love the Lord your God with all your heart, with all your soul, and with all your mind. This is the first and greatest commandment."* If we really do love Him with all our heart, soul, and mind, it will result in our truly knowing Him. And if we truly know Him, we'll be wonderfully freed up to wholeheartedly worship Him. The more time we spend studying the Scriptures and building our personal relationship with God, the better able we'll be to worship and lead others to worship in ways that really matter. In order to fully and effectively express the depth and passion of our worship to God, we must first know His divine character and attributes. We must become intimately familiar with the object of our affection.

2. Know the People

"And the second is like it: 'You shall love your neighbor as yourself'" (Matthew 22:39, NKJV). Relationships: laughing when people laugh, hurting when they hurt, being there to encourage them when the heavy situations of life arise—this is how we really know the people we minister to. The worship team is not your basic pit orchestra that plays Act I, breaks for a smoke, then returns to finish the show and run out the back door when it's over. Instead, there must be a point of connection. As members of the body of Christ, the key word for us is "mingle." Through accessibility and availability, we are going to pour ourselves into the lives of others, just as Christ has done for us.

3. Know Your Chops

Once we've established a close, personal relationship with the Lord and His people, we are primed to begin to lead others in honoring Him. But wait—are we getting ahead of ourselves? What good are grandiose ideas of lofty praise and heart-stirring worship if we haven't yet spent the time to become skilled at what we do? If we don't develop our vocal and instrumental *chops*, we won't have any tools in the worship toolbox to minister with. When the time comes to build a wonderful sound to honor the Lord, we'll be scrambling— embarrassed and humiliated! It is vitally important that we "rewind and take time." We have to know our basic scales, chords, tone, rhythm, and blend. With these implements in hand, we're always ready to play (and sing) skillfully with a shout of joy!

4. Know the Tunes

Here's where we lavish gratitude on the Lord for so many available resources! Worship music has become a massive industry. Consistent with the law of supply and demand, the number of worship resources has grown exponentially. Songbooks, CDs, instructional DVDs, the Internet, and Christian radio stations are providing nonstop access to the very latest worship tunes. It's become the pleasure of the worship team to just listen and learn. We've become spoiled, in the very best of ways, as our prayers for worship on every street corner are becoming a reality. Now we can easily know the tunes and share them with those who gather to worship under our leadership. Let's never take this resource for granted!

5. Know the Destination

Finally, the secret to planning and executing an effective worship time is to know the destination. Every worship context is different. Each requires thought and prayer in the planning stages in order to be relevant in the doing. Before we plan, we must first understand what we're planning for. What is the type and size of the gathering we're leading? Is it to be an intimate home fellowship or a conference of 3,000? Most important, if there is a teaching, what is the topic and point? Will there be a time of response at the end? What kind of response? Is there to be communion, baptisms, recommitment, or commissioning? Knowing, at least generally, where the worship time is heading empowers us to plan, rehearse, and lead more effectively. This just in from the Department of Redundancy Department: "If you don't know where you're going, any road will get you there!" *"Trust in the Lord . . .and He shall direct your path!"* Proverbs 3:5a, 6b (NKJV).

I firmly believe in keeping life as uncomplicated as possible. Whenever we narrow anything down to just five basic areas, we defeat the author of confusion. If we know the Lord, the people, the chops, the tunes, and the destination, we have a solid foundation from which to launch the most profound worship times. Let's continue to enjoy and benefit from the many wonderful worship resources available to us, and at the same time remember that God is wise in our foolishness, strong in our weakness, and uses the simple things to confound the complicated! These are the true worship team essentials.

10

Let It Breathe
(and Feel the Dynamic Rise and Fall of Worship)

The Rise and Fall . . . of Worship!

OK. Don't become overly concerned by the title. God is still on the throne. Christ remains King and salvation is forever. These don't change, but some things do, and contemporary worship belongs in that changing category. Now I'm not referring to new songs or styles. What I mean is, the experience of praise and worship is dynamic. It's in the moment. It reflects the collective heart of the people, and the leadership partnering of the Holy Spirit with the worship team.

Dynamic worship can begin quietly enough, with the low rumble of the kick drum, bass guitar, and keyboard. Then suddenly the entire band breaks forth into unbridled expressions of explosive praise, being ever mindful not to spook the congregation in the process.

Let's remember that bodies of worshipers are not organizations, they are organisms.

Just as Jehoshaphat did in II Chronicles 20:18, 19, one moment we may have our faces on the floor in worship, the next we're standing to praise the Lord with voices loud and high. This is the experience of worship dynamics! It's those moments when the demographic of the worshipers, and the style and approach of their leader, can facilitate a massive expressional swing. Let's remember that bodies of worshipers are not organizations, they are organisms. Like the amoeba, the shape and contour of the worship and the worshipers is constantly in flux. Worship breathes. It's always changing.

The Rise

In classical terms, it's a *crescendo*. In theatrical or literary lingo, it's a *climax*. And if you happen to be in a garage band, you *turn it up to 11!* No matter what language of music you speak, praise and worship reflects the ebb and flow of the creation around us. Like all things on earth, praise and worship times move pretty much in one of two directions: up or down. (OK, sideways if you're a fiddler crab on the beach.)

The rising component of worship is usually labeled "praise." These times can be characterized by moments when shouts of "hallelujah!" erupt among the people. Sometimes an overflow of exuberance in the electrically charged presence of God occurs. When His presence is palpable, His people may find it difficult to contain their responses. (See King David in II Samuel Chapter 6, specifically verses 14–16 and 21–23.)

> *Facilitating opportunities for emotive expression to God is what worship music ministry is all about.*

Ways to Raise

Arrangement, arrangement, arrangement. The live version of Hillsong's "Mighty to Save" is a great example of an arrangement rise. It begins almost as cat and mouse, with some intensity in the intro. But before you can get settled with the strength, the bottom drops out in verse 1 with pretty much an acoustic-guitar-and-vocals-only treatment. Nowhere to go but up. Brilliant. From there the instrumentation builds gradually, adding bass, more drums, keys, and electric guitar. By the time we've arrived at "Shine your light and let the whole world see," the place is coming unglued with the glory of God. Facilitating opportunities for emotive expression to God is what worship music ministry is all about, and arrangement is a key element in facilitation.

Song to Song

Another effective way to raise our praise is to link songs together that complement one another in topic, tempo, and intensity. We've just finished singing "Mighty to Save," ending on a gigantic E power chord. The congregation is on its feet, hands and voices raised to the heavens, ready to move the worship up another notch. A sudden thump, thump, thump, thump of the kick drum and bass guitar in the key of G begins. Anticipation builds as the people wait to hear what direction they're headed in. Suddenly the worship leader breaks the tension with a vocal entrance: "Great is Your faithfulness, O God . . ." And we're off again into another powerfully anointed praise song: "Your grace is enough fo-or me!"

A Pivotal Moment

In almost every praise and worship set there is a pivotal moment. It's a kind of gear shift from five-speed overdrive praise into a lower, but often more powerful, first or second worship gear. As previously mentioned, a moderate-tempo song can be placed between the faster, more boisterous praise and the slower, quieter worship. This facilitates a smooth transition, and helps to keep the shock level of the worship gear shift to a minimum.

Now let me suggest another method to smooth out those transitional bumps and bring us from high praise to intimate worship. Why not repeat the chorus of one of the faster songs you've already sung, but with a new, slower, more relaxed feel? This, like the hook of a great hit song, drives home the main theme of the worship time through repetition, and sets up the move into the slower worship songs to follow. Shall we give it a try?

We began by singing "Mighty to Save." We ended that song on a huge E power chord and took off into "Your Grace Is Enough." After finishing "Your Grace Is Enough," why not double back to the chorus of "Mighty to Save," this time in the key of G? Sing it at a moderate to slow tempo, and begin to make the worship proclamation: "Our God is mighty to save, He is (You are) mighty to save!" End the song this time on a G chord instead of E, and you're poised to seamlessly flow into a time of deeper, more personal worship expression.

The Fall

"As morning dawns and evening fades, You inspire songs of praise . . . Your name is a strong and mighty tower" (from "Your Name" by Paul Baloche). Now we're in the key of B-flat (guitarists, you may cheat by using your capo on the third fret and playing the chords as though you're in the key of G). We're ready for delicate worship, and deep, heartfelt communication with God, facilitating the expression of His Divine attributes, mixed with thankfulness for His revealing Himself in such personal ways to us.

> *How marvelous is our creator, who made us emotional beings, then facilitated the release of those emotions to Him through the perpetual rise and fall of worship!*

Once again, arrangement plays an important part in setting the mood for this type of worship interaction, without manipulation. Our instrumentation is sparse now: acoustic guitar, keyboard pads, and cellos if you've got 'em. Musically interpretive words like *vulnerable* and *transparent* come to mind. Sounds that warm and enfold the heart are emanating from the stage. The people are responding from the very core of their being: "Nothing has the power to save, but Your name."

The final chord lingers, sustained to the nth degree. It gradually fades away. The praise and worship has risen and fallen, kinetic in its ever-changing manifestation. The worship team takes a deep breath and looks around the stage into each another's eyes. They nod and smile. A peaceful sense of completion and having met with God prevails. That's the dynamic rise and fall of worship.

How marvelous is our Creator, who made us emotional beings, then facilitated the release of those emotions to Him through the perpetual rise and fall . . . of worship!

11

Improvise
(by Inspiration of the
Holy Spirit)

Improvisation by Inspiration

In 1981, the Lord blew my musical comfort zone to pieces! He called me into worship ministry. I was excited, but there was one little problem: I had never actually led worship before, at least not in that free-flowing style of worship we sometimes take for granted today. God was asking me to lead others into worship, and I was petrified. For five years I had been writing and performing Christian music in churches, but I had never experienced the awesome freedom of worshiping God with every fiber of my musical being. That was about to change . . .

> *When the Church is inspired to improvise, we begin to reflect the creative nature of a praiseworthy God.*

About six months into my first year as a worship leader, the responses of the people really began to escalate during our worship times. Their hearts became soft and pliable. During worship, their faces fairly beamed with the glory and peace of the Lord. This precious sight is etched into my mind forever. It's one of my favorite memories. It seemed that every worship time was bringing us closer to God and each other.

As our worship team grew in musical skills and spiritual sensitivity, we began to express our worship selves to the Lord with greater freedom and confidence. We weren't glued to the song list anymore. Instead, we were free to move into, out of, and between the programmed praise with times of inspired worship. I guess you could call it improvisation by inspiration. It's like jamming on a blues tune, but the soloing is stirred up in the heart of the worship musician by the Holy Spirit. The improvisation becomes a musical offering lifted up to God!

By Inspiration

Improvisation by inspiration occurs when we combine the free flow of worship with technical musical knowledge. This type of spiritual musicianship only happens when we freely abandon our musical expression to the leadership of the Holy Spirit. Egos and inhibitions are banished in favor of a much greater eternal purpose: bringing ultimate glory to God.

> "Moreover David and the captains of the army separated for the service some of the sons of Asaph, of Heman, and of Jeduthun, who should prophesy [improvise by inspiration] with harps, stringed instruments, and cymbals. And the number of the skilled men performing their service was . . . two hundred and eighty-eight."
> —I Chronicles 25:1 and 7b (NKJV)

We see from the above verse that the sons of Asaph, Heman, and Jeduthun combined the free flow of their worship (they prophesied on their instruments) with their technical musical knowledge (they were skilled at what they played). Though it may sound like an oxymoron, I believe they were exercising prophetic skills. You may ask, "How can one develop skills to do something that is by nature spiritual and flows by inspiration of the Holy Spirit?" The skills we're talking about are the earthly ones: reading, writing, singing, and playing. But the inspiration to use those skills in a prophetic manner, ministering to the Lord and His body, comes from God.

"For prophecy never came by the will of man, but holy men of God spoke as they were moved by the Holy Spirit."

—II Peter 1:21 (NKJV)

Although these holy men of God were moved to prophecy by the Spirit, they had developed certain communication skills beforehand. When the time came to hear from God, they were ready—able to understand by the Spirit and communicate God's Word to the world around them. In order for us to improvise by inspiration, we must do the same: develop communication skills with our respective voices and instruments, then allow the Lord to speak musically through us as we're inspired by the Holy Spirit.

The more you know, the better you flow!

Guidelines for Inspired Improvisation

As ethereal as all this sounds, there is a practical side to this spiritual subject. Here are a few tips that will help us to set the worship team free to improvise unto the Lord. Apply these, and you'll worship with confidence, flowing with inspiration from song to song. Remember, you can improvise over virtually any chord progression (even over one chord). Just stay relaxed, trust God, and allow the music to flow from the innermost depths of worship expression in your heart!

1. Really know your instrument.

Learn and practice scales, modes, and other relevant techniques that will give you lots of musical tools to work with. Use these to build powerful, anointed musical expressions to the Lord. The more you know, the better you flow!

2. Less is still more.

Don't try to fill every musical hole with your solo. Instead, leave space, and make time for others to be expressive in their soloing as well. During improvisation, take turns within the team, giving each member the opportunity to express what the Lord is stirring in their hearts. Don't be a *lick hog!*

3. Phrase as though you are singing.

A solo is not just a barrage of notes lobbed at the listener. It's a carefully executed series of phrases with musical breaths in between. Play like a singer, and the listener will relate.

Music is an emotional medium. Bring your instrument to tears!

4. Be musically relevant.

Appropriateness is always the order of the day. If the song is upbeat and rockin', let 'er rip! If it's more of a quiet, throne-room sort of tune, gently caress every note until you bring your instrument to tears. Music is an emotional medium.

5. Spend plenty of time with God!

Pray, study the Scriptures (especially the Psalms), and practice worshiping with your team. It's improvisation by inspiration. There's only one place to get a fresh supply of that—in the presence of God.

Inspired improvisation, interspersed with programmed songs, can be a powerfully motivating tool in the repertoire of the worship team. Improvisation allows for spontaneous creativity during worship times. It tightens the worship team and at the same time frees up the congregation. When the church is inspired to improvise, we begin to reflect the creative nature of a praiseworthy God.

Are You Lifting Up Encomiums?

1. Is it possible to lift up *encomiums* without ever singing or saying a word?
2. Is it possible to lift up encomiums just by playing your instrument, humming, dancing, or even strumming a rhythm on the Venetian blinds in the dining room? (Dust first!)
3. Is it possible that you have no earthly idea what encomiums are?

From the Top

Al-righty then, from the top. Encomiums are limitless. They span space and time. They can exist in any state or medium, and probably even in a vacuum. They are always in fashion (and never need ironing!). They can be sung, strummed, hummed, or pounded out on the most primitive of percussion. They will exist forever.

To better understand their nature, let's begin by reading selections from II Samuel 6 (NKJV), starting with verse 5. Here's the scene: David and the chosen men of Israel have just brought the ark out of the house of Abinadab. Apparently, a spontaneous praise-jam session erupts among them (how cool is that?):

"Then David and all the house of Israel played music before the Lord on all kinds of instruments made of fir wood, on harps, on stringed instruments, on tambourines, on sistrums [metal shakers], *and on cymbals."*

They were probably just gettin' their groove on when, in a moment of fatal reaction, poor Uzzah put out his hand and touched the ark. God was greatly angered by this, and *zap!*—exit Uzzah! Needless to say, David was quite shaken by this sudden, unexpected turn of events, but on the rebound, the ark was eventually brought to the City. That's when the king himself was inspired to bust a move: he *"danced before the Lord with all his might,"* and it says that he was *"leaping and whirling before the Lord!"* (verses 14 and 16). This has everything to do with encomiums!

En·co·mi·ums

So what are encomiums? Encomiums are high praises offered and expressed to the Lord. They are glowing and warmly enthusiastic, according to Merriam-Webster. They are accolades, commendations, homages, and tributes of all sizes, shapes, forms, configurations, intensities, and eccentricities. Throughout our lives they can come from the valleys or the mountaintops, the skies over L.A. or the depths of the sea. Encomiums are always appropriate: at any time, in any place, and from anyone. They express our deepest, least inhibited, heartfelt desire to bring glory to God.

Praising God with Bubbles

I love to scuba dive. Underwater caves, peaceful and awe-inspiring, have often been my dive destinations. Imagine diving to 60 feet, swimming into a gaping, pitch-black hole and, with only the narrow beam of your dive light, making your way into the flooded bowels of the earth. There, you turn out all the lights (absolute darkness surrounds you), set your buoyancy vest to neutral buoyancy, and like an unborn baby still safe in his mother's womb, hang weightless in inner space. You rise slightly with each inhale and move in the opposite direction as you breathe out. *Ahhhhhhh.* Sweet peace and total immersion in the presence of God! You're in His arms now, and as He gently rocks you in this mysterious subterranean version of Sea World, you spontaneously begin to hum His praises. With every breath you take you can hear the hiss of compressed air passing from your second-stage regulator into your lungs. But the worship payoff comes as you exhale. You become acutely aware of the sound of your own humming bubbles lifting up encomiums to the Lord in the most unlikely place on earth! You're offering glowing, warmly enthusiastic scuba-diving praise!

The Jonah Factor

Scuba praise? Does that sound a bit far-fetched or unbelievable? "No Biblical precedent," you say? Think again. From Jonah 2:7 (NKJV): *"When my soul fainted within me, I remembered the Lord; and my prayer went up to You, into Your holy temple."* These words weren't exactly offered up from the comfort of Jonah's favorite easy chair in front of the widescreen TV at his house. On the contrary, as we say in scuba lingo, he was *at depth*. He was way under water, and to complicate matters, inside the belly of a very large fish! And yet his thoughts and prayers were of and to the Lord. Anywhere, any time, from anyone!

Encomiastic Responses

Worship, led by a team or otherwise, is more than what we do on Sunday morning for 30 to 45 minutes at the beginning of each service. It's a lifestyle, a response to spiritual stimuli, and just like our musical skills, it requires practice. Encomiums need to become an almost involuntary response to all our life situations. The question is, how do we program ourselves for the kind of responses we saw in King David or Jonah?

Three Ways to Instant Praise

Just what does it take to become an "I.E.L." (instant encomium lifter)? How do we develop the habit of high praises? As in the acquisition of any other worthwhile trait, we practice, practice, practice!

1. Practice meditating on the Scriptures.

This one is from David himself, as inspired by the Holy Spirit. *"But his delight is in the law of the Lord. And in His law he meditates day and night."* Psalm 1:2 (NKJV) again! What a beautiful picture. Just imagine chewing on the Word all day and all night. Spontaneous praises in multiple forms most certainly begin to flow from your lips and life when you do!

2. Practice being thankful.

Practice being thankful for everything that comes your way. One of my all-time favorite worship songs, "Come Fall on Us," by Ben & Robin Pasley of 100 Portraits, has a bridge that begins with "A thankful heart prepares the way for You, my God." Only the Lord Himself could have said it better, and when He did, He coupled it with *"always rejoice,"* and *"don't stop praying."* We are then instructed in I Thessalonians 5:16-18 (NKJV) to *"give thanks in everything because it's God's will for us."*

3. Practice being a living sacrifice.

Practice being a living sacrifice to the Lord, which Romans 12:1 says is our *"reasonable act of worship."* We praise Him, lifting up encomiums for every chance to decrease so that He may increase. (In everything give thanks.)

Today you've learned a new word and many of its expressions. It is my prayer that this new word, *encomiums,* will now inspire you to new acts of worship you never even dreamed of! As believers, worship is our forever life, and the worship life is all about—you guessed it—encomiums!

Praise Beyond the Songs

We've all heard that inner voice before, during worship. It's the one insisting that there's more; more to worship than we're experiencing. We identify with that voice, and recognize the deep longing in our hearts. We desire to be set free in worship, to offer our very own praise to God. Uninhibited by structure or form, voices raised, faces turned in the direction of heaven, we ascend with clean hands and a pure heart ". . . *into the hill of the Lord*" (Psalm 24:3, 4). In our mind's ear we can hear waves of worship crashing at the feet of Jesus. We feel the salty wind of the Spirit carrying us where He will. The sands of the promised land are between our toes. It all sounds so fantastic and ethereal. Can we really get there from here? Is it possible to know the flow of praise beyond the songs?

Free Worship Gridlock

Rather than flowing freely, our worship times often resemble stop-and-go traffic. We play the first song, then stop. We start the next song, then stop again. Maybe we pray or read a Scripture, then we start playing, stop, start, stop, start. In order for our teams to ever break free of this bumper-to-bumper mode, we need to drive for a while on a smooth, straight highway of corporate worship, coursing through wide-open spaces of personal praise.

The Highway

The highway of worship I'm referring to is represented by our predetermined worship sets. These include our praise and worship songs, programmed prayers, responsive readings, inspirational video clips, worship dramas, dance, Scriptures, and the other elements we've planned out before the actual worship time begins. With proper training and practice, the skills needed to plan an effective worship set list can be acquired, then honed to a high proficiency level. This is the well-paved road that solid corporate worship travels on.

The Wide-Open Spaces

The spaces are another thing altogether. While the worship highway gives us a stable, predictable road to follow from the beginning to the end of a worship time, the wide-open spaces surrounding the highway give us the opportunity for the free flow of personal and corporate worship. Our worship should breathe, exhibiting a healthy mixture of programmed and spontaneous elements. As much as we love and embrace the latest worship songs from our favorite worship leaders/writers, I believe that nothing compares to freely expressed praises springing from the hearts of *off the road* congregational worshipers!

> *We must not allow the wheels of worship to become
> stuck in the rut of routine!*

Creating the Space

What if we break out of some of our worship time ruts and begin to search diligently for the wide-open spaces? If you're ready to give it a try, here are some tips to help take us from the safe, smooth highway of predictability into the unexplored country of inspired praise.

1. Free Worship Chord Progressions

As mentioned earlier, the free worship chord progression is probably the most common device for facilitating improvised worship during an already programmed worship time (see Chapter 7: Find the Flow). A worship song usually makes a broad, general statement of praise or adoration to God. But at times we may feel the need to be more specific or personal than the lyrical expressions of the composer. This is where free worship chord progressions seem to serve best.

By ending a worship song with an oft-repeated chord progression, we allow the worshiper time to offer individual praises and thanksgiving. We should flow smoothly from the end of the song into the free worship chord progression.

Free worship chord progressions usually mirror the most common chord sequence within the preceding song. If the tune is in the key of E and is using a chord progression such as E – A2 – B4 – A2, it is easy to continue repeating the progression at the end of the song, thereby providing the worshipers the opportunity to offer their personal praises. Then, when the moment is right, we simply move on to the next programmed song.

2. Alpha and Omega Songs

This suggestion is a bit risky, but a wonderful facilitator of free worship. Let me challenge you, just this once, to plan a worship time with only a beginning song and an ending song (alpha and omega), and nothing in between. "What do I do with all that space?" you ask. That's between you, the team, and God. Why not try this at a worship team rehearsal first? Open with prayer, hand out the charts for the two alpha and omega tunes, then ask the team to trust the Holy Spirit with you for whatever happens in the middle. As long as it is Christ-honoring, it's a good thing. If it works well at rehearsal, take it up a notch to the congregation and watch what the Lord will do.

3. Worship Without Words

In 1995, the Youth with a Mission School of Music in Missions found itself on the border between Germany and the Netherlands. We were attending the historic "In Your Presence" Worship Festival, celebrating the 50th anniversary of the end of World War II. This was the first time we had ever experienced "worship without words." The rules were simple enough:

1. No words (except prophetic songs or sung Scriptures).
2. It's OK to hum, la, play rhythms, play instruments, dance, whirl, leap, bow, lift up hands, etc.
3. Any sound except for words is acceptable.
4. Silence is acceptable.

We were amazed as the worship team began to play chordal progressions with solo improvisations. They encouraged the corporate body to begin to honor God in whatever ways they were inspired. There were no charts, and little structure, but the worship times flowed smoothly from the inspiration of the Holy Spirit. Those in attendance expressed their praises in a myriad of ways, including playing rhythms on the backs of metal chairs and humming the most heavenly melodies. Since then, some of the sweetest and most sincere worship I have ever experienced has been without words.

As worship leaders/followers, we must not allow the wheels of worship to become stuck in the rut of routine! Our God is first the Creator, and we have His permission to exercise that wonderful gift of creativity in worship ourselves. It is our never-ending privilege to discover new ways to praise Him—beyond the songs!

Even Your Prayers Can Praise

Let my cry come right into Your presence, God . . .
Let praise cascade off my lips . . .
And let Your promises ring from my tongue . . .
Invigorate my soul so I can praise You well . . .

—From Psalm 119:169-175 (*The Message Remix*, by Eugene H. Peterson)

What a prayer! Every word of every line should literally thrill the heart of the true worshiper! God's promises ringing from our tongues? Praise cascading off our lips? Just imagine!

Ponder for a moment praises, like the never-ending torrents of Niagara Falls, overflowing from us into eternity. Can you see yourself in this picture? The very thought should make us ravenous for worship. Let's shout it together, "God, invigorate my soul so I can praise You well!" Now once more with feeling: "God, invigorate my soul so I can praise You well!!" These were once King David's words, inspired by the Holy Spirit. They now belong to you.

Divine Design

It's amazing how the Lord created us with a God-shaped void in our hearts and a praise-shaped void in our mouths. He knew first that we must accept in our hearts the salvific work of Jesus Christ on the cross. But afterward, He also knew that praying our praises, and praising Him with our prayers, would draw us closer to Him. Faith is enriched when our mouths proclaim His character and Divine attributes. The relationship to our Heavenly Father grows when the beliefs in our hearts and the confessions of our mouths are in alignment. We read in Mark 11:24 (NKJV), "*Therefore I say to you, whatever things you ask when you pray, believe that you receive them, and you will have them.*" When our mouth is praying, and our heart is believing simultaneously, things just start to *happen* in our lives. We begin to enjoy answered prayers. And because we're praising as we pray, God gets all the glory. How cool is that? It's an obvious Divine design, set in motion to bring God glory, and bring us peace and victory while we live on this earth. I marvel.

A Thessalonian Sandwich

I Thessalonians 5:16-18 (NKJV) reads like a recipe for a praise/prayer/praise sandwich: *16. "Rejoice always"* (praise); *17. "pray without ceasing"* (prayer); *18. "in everything give thanks;* (praise) *for this is the will of God in Christ Jesus for you."* We live, rejoicing in the goodness of God, praying constantly according to what the Scriptures say about Him, then thanking Him in every situation, knowing that He got there before we did! (What a relief.) When this type of praise/prayer/praise practice pervades, incredible things are bound to happen.

With this in mind, let's also remember that there's a huge difference between praying "Lord, please help me," and praying/praising "Lord, You alone are able to help me." The former is totally me-centered: "Help me, help me!" But in the second example, we're focusing not on our personal need for help, but on God's ability to provide the help we need. We're actually engaged in praising Him for His ability. Praying this way not only builds our faith, but acknowledges His Divine power to do what He says He'll do. He's able, and as we pray with praise instead of wants and needs, we become acutely aware of His infinite ability as He answers.

Prayers of Praise

Layer One

Let's discuss *three layers of prayers* including praise. We begin with the personal. As a worship team leader, I find that the entire process of planning weekly worship goes much better when it's bathed in praising prayers. Prayers from Proverbs, for example, that God will direct my steps as I prepare (Proverbs 16:9) are often spoken during the planning time. As the song list for the week materializes, so do my prayers of praise for His inspiration and anointing of the upcoming corporate worship.

Layer Two

The second layer of prayers of praise occurs when *"two or three* (usually the worship team) *are gathered together in His name . . ."* During weekly communications and worship rehearsals, prayers of praise are lifted up in acknowledgment of His presence and power. As we gather for weekly rehearsal, the team takes time to rejoice together in what God has done, and to thank Him in advance for His goodness and mercy in our lives and worship times.

Team prayers of praise again are offered just before we lead the body of Christ in worship. We deeply desire to see the Lord moving and ministering in the lives of His people, and since He's already promised to do that, we simply need to thank Him for it in advance.

Layer Three

Our final layer of prayer is our corporate prayers of praise. How awesome it is to hear the collective voice of God's people reciting His words in unified prayer. The Scripture says we're to *"remember His marvelous works which He has done,"* and *"make known His deeds among the people."* Here's our chance! With careful planning, Scriptures of prayer and praise can be interspersed between the songs in our worship list and read in unison. Liturgical readings and original prayers of praise can also be used to support the central worship theme of the day.

This weekly numerical prayer-build from personal to small group to large corporate gathering adds an element of anticipation to the worship-planning process. Every week our excitement grows as we move toward that moment when the body of Christ will come together once again to affirm our love for Him, and rehearse His incredible, unfathomable sacrifices for us. As the Scripture says, *"Let my cry come right into Your presence, God!"* With intentionality, let me purpose my prayers to bring You praise!

12

Meant to Multiply
(Giving Your Secrets Away)

Putting the "Meant to" in the *Mentor*

It just happened again! It was "Bye-bye Mike," this time. It could just as easily have been Ryan or Raymond or RJ or Matt or Mark or Jen or . . . you get the picture. Somebody's gone. History has repeated itself. Gone. A person I believed in, encouraged, and equipped to be their very best in a life of worship ministry. A protégé, a *mentee*, a 21st-century disciple. Someone I learned that I could depend upon to offer consistent, quality contributions to the weekly worship ministry. Someone who could competently stand in the gap in my absence. Now they're gone at the behest of One whose plan supersedes my own. My scheme to get everything on the worship team working just perfectly, then freeze it in perpetuity, appears to have been askew. Why does it seem that those in whom we have invested the most are often the most likely to be Divinely relocated? Perhaps it's because they've been properly prepared, and the Lord is now ready to release them into His greater plan for their lives and the lives of others they'll impact. I'd really like to think that's it!

The departure of someone we've helped to grow into a vital worship ministry partner can be a real head-scratcher! The good news? Oftentimes the joy of seeing a protégé released into a ministry of their own far outweighs the pain of letting them go!

125

Out of a Job

During the most grueling worship ministry interview I can remember, I made a comment that very nearly cost me the job opportunity. When asked about some of my goals for personal worship ministry, I answered that my number-one goal was to always be working myself out of the job. I found out later that the board simply didn't grasp that concept. This very nearly disqualified me from the candidate list. As Ricky Ricardo used to say on *I Love Lucy*, I had some *'splainin'* to do! My potential employers needed to understand what it meant to "work myself out of the job." I looked to the Gospel for the *'splaination.*

In the Book of John 4:34, 35 (NKJV): *"Jesus said to them, My food is to do the will of Him who sent Me, and to finish His work. Do you not say, 'There are yet four months and then comes the harvest?' Behold, I say to you, lift up your eyes and look at the fields, for they are already white for harvest!"* In verse 38a, Jesus follows with: *"I sent you to reap . . ."*

In these verses, there are obvious steps that the Lord takes in the process of working Himself out of His earthly job.

First, He stated clearly that "[His job was] *to do the will of Him who sent* [Him] . . ."

After this, He demonstrated to the disciples how to get the job done through His use of miracles, teaching, debating, and living love.

Next, He worked alongside them, encouraging them to see for themselves the *"white fields ready for harvest."* This step allowed the disciples to begin to take ownership of the job themselves, while still giving them the safety net of Jesus's physical presence.

Finally, He *"sent them to reap . . ."* He released them to do the job they'd been prepared for. Jesus taught by example, then freely allowed others to assume the job He was performing on earth. His position as God/man was not threatened by empowering others to participate with Him in the mission He had already begun!

Hindrance Schmindrance!

In some way or other, even if you're not the designated leader, you can become a great mentor, releasing members of the worship team you're serving into the full use of their gifts. Good mentors, disciplers, managers, and trainers seem to have at least one wonderful thing in common: they are always working to raise up others, encouraging them to equal or exceed their own level of expertise. The heart's desire of a mentor should be to help the mentee develop the tools he or she requires to rise to the heights of his or her abilities. The mentees are then released to do what they were created to do, secure in the knowledge that they've been believed in, invested in, befriended, and encouraged by someone who's pulling for their ultimate success.

The greatest hindrance to this type of input into the lives of others (you may already have guessed) is pride! Jesus's authority was not threatened by empowering others. If we live in fear of losing our own position as the best, most professional, expert king of the hill, we can begin to imagine a threat to our worship turf. Worst-case scenario, we may even suffer from what I would call "paralytic procrastination." This basically means that we become like a deer in the headlights, frozen in our own tracks by our desire to stay on top!

But look at the heart of Jesus as He encouraged His disciples in John 14:12b (NKJV): "*. . . the works that I do* [you] *will do also; and greater works than these* [you] *will do . . .*" We can see that pride never entered His picture; just the sheer pleasure of seeing others released into their full, godly potential. This is the true heart of a mentor!

Content to Ment'

Every time I return from the annual Worship Mentors Network Gathering (www .worshipmentor.com), I am more determined than ever that I must continue to always be working myself out of my job by raising up others! How about you? Wouldn't it be cool to become an intentional investor in the lives of those the Lord leads to you? Could it be that you are meant to mentor? If your answer is yes, here are four fundamental steps to help you get started:

1. Identify potential mentees through observation and conversation, resulting in personal revelation.
2. Approach the potential mentee and present the possibility of mentorship.
3. Relate with the mentee on multiple levels. Emphasize listening first (on your part), then speaking. Remember: God created us with two ears and one mouth!
4. Release the mentee to *"be what they be!"* Just as Jesus did, send them out to reap, fully knowing that they are never really alone.

Identify, approach, relate, and release. These four points, coupled with your heart's desire to serve and encourage others, will enable you to put the "meant to" in your mentorship.

No longer will your investment in others be by happenstance. Instead, you will become intentional, instigating input infused with Divine inspiration and the wisdom of godly instruction. Yes, it will break your heart to see them go. But you'll wave good-bye knowing that they're taking a part of you with them into a future that God has prepared!

Appendix A:
10 Top Tips for Tight Teams
(Guaranteed to Change Your Worship Life)

Live the Life

The life of a worshiper is manifest in two ways. First, we check our hearts. According to Psalm 24, they should be pure and never lifted up to an idol. Our hearts define the god we serve (worship). To have any other god before Him is a breach of the first and greatest commandment. Living the life requires a moment-by-moment heart check, ensuring that only the True God receives our praise through every thought, word, and action.

Then we take a look at our hands. What are they doing for the Lord? As the state of our heart determines whom we serve, the works of our hands proclaim our identity to the world around us. To live the life of a worshiper, we keep our hearts pure before the Lord, and our hands busy doing the works that glorify Him! This is the mission, in some form or other, of every true worshiper.

Worship Warm

Remember that old Thanksgiving hymn, "Now Thank We All Our God"? How about the lyrics in the second line, "With heart and hands and voices"? These are the three areas where we worship warm. The heart must stay pliable before God, always prepared to repent in humility before Him. Our hands and voices stay ready through proper rest, exercise, and warm-up routines to bring Him glory at a moment's notice.

Get Out of the Garage

How do we stop sounding like a garage band and move toward a more professional presentation? We can begin by upgrading to higher-quality gear. Then, tune the team with an electronic tuner. Most important, remember that less is more. Using sparse song arrangements is probably the fastest way to move from the garage to Carnegie Hall! (See you there!)

Sing like a Sandwich

Yes sir, two delicious pieces of whole wheat with a luscious slab of Grade-A roast beef in the middle. *Mmm-mmm.* That's the way to sing! For tight, contemporary vocal harmonies, think of it this way: The beef represents the melody line. A third above the beef is whole-wheat slice #1. Whole wheat slice #2 is also actually above the melody, a fifth, but we have to drop it an octave because a sandwich looks really dumb with two pieces of bread together and the beef underneath. After the octave drop, we're singing a first inversion of the chord. Spelled 5, 1, 3, it's the recipe for vocal harmonic success!

Check the Chart

I'll say it one more time (and please forgive the redundancy): If you don't know where you're going, any road will get you there. Whether you're using a chord/lyric sheet, lead sheet, or just a simple chord chart, check it. The worship team should always follow the road map together. How else will they know when they've arrived?

Find the Flow

Seamless worship is defined as worship that flows from one song to the next, with no stops in between. This seamless flow happens when we link worship songs together with intervals of personal or corporate free worship. The link? Free worship chord progressions between songs.

Make the Mod (Modulation)

Avoid a musical train wreck by ensuring that everyone on the team changes key together!

Lead and Be Led

The worship leader/follower must first listen for God's heart, then be anxious to point the people in His direction. Our worship check list should include: being spiritually prepared (remember to worship warm), creating master song lists by tempo (praise, then worship), then moving keys steadily up the scale from song to song during worship times, always in the direction of Heaven.

Let It Breathe

During corporate worship, the team should be dynamic (loud and soft) and diverse (fast and slow), with sprinkles of free worship and personal expression to God. Remember to let it breathe and enjoy the rise and fall of worship—together.

Improvise (by Inspiration)

Improvisation by inspiration occurs when we combine our technical musical knowledge with free-flowing worship. We learn our chops, and spend plenty of time with God, always remembering that it's improvisation by inspiration, and there's only one place to get a fresh supply of that!

Appendix B:
31 Ways to Praise
(Rx for Worshiper's Block)

No matter how exuberantly worshipful we are, at some point in our worship lives we may find ourselves coming down with a rare and painful disease peculiar to those in the praise profession. It doesn't matter if we're the lead worshiper or the background piccolo puffer—this malady can seriously affect the way we *do* worship.

You find yourself standing before the people with glazed eyes. Stupefied and confused, you wonder why you even showed up. Your palms begin to sweat. Your voice quavers. In desperation you shake your head and begin to ask yourself nonsensical questions like, "Are you sure King David started out this way?" That's when you know. All doubt has disappeared. The symptoms are too specific: you've contracted the dreaded *worshiper's block*! If you're the one responsible for leading others in the awesome activity of glorifying God, you'd probably rather wake up with full-blown flu.

The Cause

"But how did this happen?" you ask. "It seems like only yesterday I was passionate, focused, and totally in love with loving Jesus. Now I'm as dry as a bone. I feel like I've never worshiped in my life. Inconceivable!"

Actually, it's quite conceivable. As worshipers, we live on the *front lines* (see II Chronicles 20:21). We have an enemy who mimics a roaring lion, and he's seeking those he may devour—us! It's that old inventory principle they teach in business math: first in, first out. Life's circumstances bring with them multiple opportunities for worshiper's block. Instead of bringing us to our knees before the Lord, the worship leadership issues we deal with can sometimes make us feel like standing up and walking out. When challenged with poor worship team relational dynamics, fears, health issues, or personal sins, we can find our worship selves dancing with disaster!

But don't despair! We serve a God who is faithful and consistent, always ready to reignite the dwindling flames of worship passion. No matter what the circumstance, there is a cure for worshiper's block. And like vitamin C, it must be taken every day!

Getting Over It!

First, we deal directly with the problem. If it's sin, repent. Relationship issues? Reconcile. Fear? Perfect love casts it out! Take whatever steps are necessary to begin the restoration process. In so doing, you remove the barriers to worshiping in Spirit and truth. Action breaks the barrier between you and God.

Next, the prescription: 31 Ways to Praise. Take one way per day upon rising, for as long as symptoms persist! David said in the Psalms, *"I will bless the Lord at all times, His praise will continually be on my lips."* The Lord has instructed us to *"rejoice always . . . and give thanks in everything."* It's a Divine paradox that we overcome worshiper's block by worshiping! In Figure B-1, appearing in alphabetical order, are 31 ways to praise. I encourage you to focus on one way each day, starting all over again at the beginning of each month.

If your word for today is serve (#23), then in every thought, word, and deed, serve the Lord. If it's magnify (#15), try to magnify God in every way all day. We don't become highly skilled worship musicians by being lazy. We practice and practice until we nail it. The same goes for developing a worship lifestyle. We gotta work on it 'til we get it right. A daily dose of praise will help us to stay spiritually healthy and mentally focused. It's just the right medicine for preventing worshiper's block!

Figure Appendix B-1

ASCRIBE Ps. 68:34 1	BLESS Ps. 34:1 2	BOAST Ps. 34:2 3	COME Ps. 100:2 4	DELIGHT Ps. 37:4 5	EXALT Ps. 99:9 6	FEAR Ps. 34:9 7
GLORIFY Rom. 15:6 8	HONOR Prov. 3:9 9	HUMBLE James 4:10 10	IMITATE 1 Cor.11:1 11	JOY Hab. 3:18 12	KNEEL Ps. 95:6 13	LOVE Ps. 31:23 14
MAGNIFY Ps. 34:3 15	(Draw) NEAR James 4:8 16	OFFER Heb. 13:15 17	PRAISE Ps. 35:18 18	QUIET Ps. 131:2 19	REJOICE Phil. 4:4 20	REMEMBER Ps. 105:5 21
SACRIFICE Jonah 2:9 22	SERVE Ps. 100:2 23	SUBMIT James 4:7 24	TELL Ps. 9:1 25	UTTER Ps. 145:7 26	VOW Deut. 23:23 27	WAIT Is. 40:31 28
(E)XTOL Ps. 145:1 29	YIELD 2 Chrn. 30:8 30	(Be) ZEALOUS Titus 2:14 31	**31 WAYS TO PRAISE** (One-Way-Per-Day) NKJV			

Index I:
List of Terms for Tips

Index II: List of Scripture References

Worship Musician!™
PRESENTS
Series

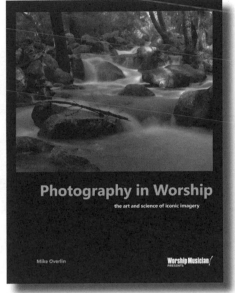

Tips for Tight Teams

High-Performance Help
for Today's Worship Musician
by Sandy Hoffman
Hal Leonard

Tips for Tight Teams instructs and equips today's worship musician to function on the musical, relational, and technical levels expected of 21st-century worship team leaders and members. Rooted in Sandy Hoffman's "Ten Top Tips for Tight Teams" curriculum, the book covers a myriad of timeless and relevant worship topics. The goal of *Tips for Tight Teams* is to elevate skill levels to the point where the worship team is no longer a distraction to the people it endeavors to lead into worship.

$16.99 • 8-1/2" x 11" • 160 pages • Softcover
978-1-4584-0291-2

Photography in Worship

The Art and Science of Iconic Imagery
by Mike Overlin
Hal Leonard

The ability to take a photograph – to stop a moment in time – is a very powerful act in and of itself. When this skill is used in the creation of imagery in support of worship, or even as an act of worship, it can be truly breathtaking. This book will teach you the basics of photography through simple explanations and practical examples, and more important, how to "see" the image in advance, with special emphasis on creating imagery for use in worship.

$29.99 • 8-1/2" x 11" • 208 pages • Softcover
978-1-4584-0295-0

The Worship Band Book

Training and Empowering
Your Worship Band
by Tom Lane
Hal Leonard

Whether you're in a band yourself or part of a ministry involved with teams, this book can help you on your journey. Spiritual, relational, professional, and practical issues relevant for individuals and groups in worship ministry of any kind are addressed head-on. This book will help lay the foundation for a healthier pursuit of creative dreams and a closer walk with God.

$16.99 • 8-1/2" x 11" • 128 pages • Softcover
978-1-4584-1817-3

Prices, contents, and availability subject to change without notice.